THE CROSS AND ITS MEANINGLESSNESS

A Prayer *of* Final Obsolescence

TIMOTHY JOHN TRACY

Published by River Grove Books
Austin, TX
www.rivergrovebooks.com

Copyright ©2017 Timothy Tracy

All rights reserved.

Thank you for purchasing an authorized edition of this book and for complying with copyright law. No part of this book may be reproduced, stored in a retrieval system, or transmitted by any means, electronic, mechanical, photocopying, recording, or otherwise, without written permission from the copyright holder.

Distributed by River Grove Books

Design and composition by Sheila Parr
Cover design by Sheila Parr
Cover art by Jason Craighead
Author photograph by Holly Tracy
Crown rendering by Greer Miceli

Unless otherwise noted, all biblical references or quotations are taken from the Holy Bible, New International Version, copyright ©1973, 1978, 1984 by International Bible Society. Used by permission of Zondervan. All rights reserved.

Cataloging-in-Publication data is available.

Print ISBN: 978-1-63299-131-7

eBook ISBN: 978-1-63299-132-4

First Edition

To the church

Contents

Preface vii

The Beginning 1

The Inquisition 17

The Unbelief 27

The Scripture 77

The Meaning 99

The Testimony 115

The Finish 135

Glossary 161

Acknowledgments 169

About the Author 171

Preface

This prayer searches for the truth of God's character in the cross of Christ, an endless inquiry to be sure, but one within the embrace of our hearts and the reach of our minds. If we could not obtain a basic understanding of who God is, creation would have been pointless, a creation of nothing from nothing and for nothing.

The culmination of eighteen months of intense reflection, this prayer engages the traditional theological understandings of the crucifixion in search of a deeper understanding of who God was during his son's suffering, forsakenness, and death. For a year and a half of contemplation on a boat in a slough of an Alabama reservoir, I embraced two thousand years of profound Christian thought and meditation, beginning with Christ himself, then the apostolic writers, the church fathers, and many distinguished theologians who followed in their footsteps.

Some of those early church teachers lived amid political oppression and persecution so severe that to utter "I believe in Jesus Christ, my Lord and my God" yielded a one-way trip to the Roman arena. How could an abiding and rich tradition of men and women who deeply believed and deeply felt that the cross of Christ was the sole ground upon which God forgave our sin be mistaken about the meaning of the crucifixion? But, neither the sheer duration of a belief nor the fierce unwillingness to renounce it, even in the face of death, assures its truthfulness.

Why look for the truth of God's character in the cross? Why not focus on the resurrection, especially because historians earnestly contend that Christianity would not exist without belief in a risen Christ? For many Christians, the cross was the most pivotal historical event in all of Christianity and the most revelatory of who God is, the consummate act of a divine unclothing. This is not to say that the resurrection, the incarnation, or other episodes in the life of Christ are not significant, or fail to reveal God. They also show us divine ingredients that are essential for understanding God's thoughts and ways. But the crucifixion of the Son of God was where the truth of who God is in himself and the truth of who God is with us were most disclosed.

To see the cross as the core of Christianity is a particularly Protestant interpretive choice. Other events in the story of Christianity could be chosen as seminal to its message. Eastern Orthodoxy, for example, has always seen the incarnation as critical in God's revelation to humanity. Regardless of what we choose to believe is at the heart of Christianity, we're obligated to reflect on and engage the consequences of that choice, and to subject it to God, no matter how much we are attached to it. To refuse to expose our understanding of who God is to God himself is a calcified impiety.

Whatever Christianity says God was doing with Christ on the cross must be the same as what God does in eternity. The God Christianity says he was as his son was being nailed to the cross cannot be different from the God he is in eternity. His character must be the same, regardless of any time or situation, even if there were no creatures to save. To understand this truth and its infinite implications is the beginning of wisdom. To see that nothing external to God—neither you, nor me, nor our worst sin, and not even the death of his only son—can change him is the beginning of faith. To relinquish the idea that God measures our value based on the depth of Christ's agony on the cross is the beginning of freedom. Christianity has darkened the beauty of divine truth with needless explanations to secure the indispensability of the cross, explanations which have unbelief as their core.

Some in the tradition have argued that humanity, sin, and the cross are all present to God at the same time in one eternally grand moment with no duration or change. Without question, formidable challenges rapidly arise when we probe how God is in himself. But to sweep this prayer underneath a blanket of intellectual incomprehensibility does nothing more than decline to understand the truth of God. Is he good? Is he always good?

I think the message of Christianity begins wrong. It starts off with a profoundly perverted perspective of God's character. The picture of God that usually emerges only moments after Christians begin their theological explanation is not good. In fact, it's bad. The picture it presents is as if God sits comfortably on the judgment seat, shrouded in an accusatory holiness and salivating with divine delight for the day when he will condemn most of humanity with pleasure, but forgive and save the few souls who believe that God's son bore their condemnation on the cross. This is a God who, because of our corrupt, depraved, and rebellious nature, has the holy right to reject, abandon, and hate us utterly, but somehow transformed through his crucified son into a God free to bestow love, mercy, and a warm welcome upon those who look to his son's pain on the cross for their salvation. No wonder Christianity has obsessed for nearly two thousand years over the "good news." Its message begins with "bad news." But the bad news is wrong news and the good news is bad news. The truth of God's character is the beginning and end of all news.

Understanding the character of God is my obsession. I chose the form of a prayer for this book because God is obligated to listen to his creatures, an idea as true of him as it is alien to Christians who are convinced that the nature of obligation stands in hostile opposition to the nature of grace, when in fact they are one and the same. God listens to everything we say, whether true, false, unintelligible, or utter nonsense. He understands why we say or ask the things that we do, even if we don't know how to say or ask them. "And even the very hairs of your head are all numbered" (Matthew 10:30) was not a mathematical statement of Christ's but an ontological one, because every fragment of our being and experience is intimately, not covertly, known by God. So why not reason with God himself? Why not always remain open to him? Perhaps he will refute the stories that we tell about him.

It seemed fitting to begin and end my prayer with a portion of three recorded utterances of Christ while he hung on the cross: "My God, my God, why have you forsaken me" (Matthew 27:46), an utterance of forsakenness;

"Father, into your hands I commit my spirit" (Luke 23:46), an utterance of love; and "It is finished" (John 19:30), an utterance of finality. Whether my thoughts between those articulations of our dying Lord approach the truth of God is for the reader to judge.

Before reading this prayer, take a few moments and imagine yourself standing face-to-face with God himself. Imagine that no one else and no other thing are around—no family, friend, pastor, pope, or angel, and no Bible, creed, book of life, throne, or other heavenly embellishments. It's only you and God. Look deep into his eyes. What do you see? What would you say? What do you think he would say?

Note to Readers: I love words and am always searching for new or different ones to convey meaning where familiar words would work just as well. So the complex vocabulary you may see in this prayer is solely a matter of affection, not intellectual pretense. I have added a glossary at the end of this prayer for convenience.

In addition, according to a number of grammarians and linguists, the use of a singular "they" or "their" has become somewhat acceptable in formal prose. I have adopted this convention here to avoid the cumbersome alternatives required for gender neutrality.

—Timothy J. Tracy

CHAPTER 1

The Beginning

My God, my God, into thy hands I commit this prayer. Its fate will be determined in heaven as the wheat and waste on earth were gently winnowed within the open palm of perfect love—the incarnate breath of your son.

From the moment you spoke creation into existence and your timelessness began to shed time, until this moment, no event has encircled the forces of contradiction or distended the powers of paradox as much as when the blood of your only son was shed on a Roman cross. Jesus Christ, the perfect union of divinity and humanity, ended up as a crucified criminal. Why?

Your church has steadfastly proclaimed that there is

no discrepancy between the eternal truth of his divinity and the historical fact of his crucifixion. In the fullness of time after the second person of the Trinity had emptied himself by becoming flesh and blood, he went to Golgotha to shed between two other criminals the very blood he had assumed. There, he paid the price of your justice and obtained forgiveness for the world. The place where every sinner should have been was the place where Christ, in obedience to you and in love for us, died. The divine exchange was accomplished. According to the church, my sinful predilections and the actuality of my every sin had been erased from your mind because of what had happened to your son. This is what I believed for most of my life.

Not long ago, however, I began to question the traditional meanings of the cross. Why do you, in order to be merciful, need the violent suffering and death of the only innocent man? You create from pleasure, not from need. You love the world. You are love. You are sovereign over all. You are the father of everything beautiful. You are beautiful. You reign in a peaceful and perfect harmony within the Trinitarian Godhead.

Much of Christianity would agree with this description, but would insist that it is incomplete because it neglects to mention your holiness and justice. Some would contend that the description also fails to mention your wrath. With a more adequate description of your nature in hand, Christianity implores us to believe that the crucifixion of your son, together with all of his terror, suffering, and forsakenness, was a reflection of your holy and just character, the fulfillment of your righteous demands. Was it really?

I am not alone with these questions. There are Christians who would never consider a public announcement of their doubt about one of the few explicative cornerstones of Christian belief, would never dream of breaking with a tradition of such monumental proportions, but yet silently struggle with the meaning of the cross. They may nod in agreement as the clergy declares the necessity for the broken body and shed blood of your son, but their consciences recoil and tremble at the thought that you require suffering as the gateway to your eternal forgiving presence. Whether they go public or stay private with their sentiments is of no consequence to me. I understand how they feel. But I hope those Christians, as few as they may be, will come to see that their intuition of tremulous hesitancy about the purpose of the crucifixion is divine.

Speaking of gateways, the resurrection is not a corridor to a deeper understanding of your character. That corridor is lined with the dark shadows cast by the cross of Christ.

The resurrection is all light. It projects no aphotic qualities. You are the God of the living as the Scriptures testify. No one within your mind can die. I see you clearly in the resurrection. But it's not what I see that interests me. It's what I can't see. In that sense, therefore, the resurrection is almost a distraction, a deflection from the opportunity to get beneath the perplexity of the crucifixion and a move toward a narcissistic reverie of endless existence.

On the other hand, the event of the cross is full of contradiction and conflict, characteristics that mobilize and invite the heart and mind to comprehend your nature in deeper ways. It is within the darkness of the crucifixion that I desire to understand the truth of who you are. I hope this prayer encourages others to do the same, to set aside the captivation of the traditional theologies of the cross, if only for a spell, and to consider whether the truth of your character reveals a different meaning of the cross or no meaning at all.

I am familiar with those visceral objections to anyone who questions the entrenched meanings of the cross that would characterize this oblation as a reactionary invective, an insulting irreverence, or the deplorable incantations of a defector. More calculatingly perceptive reactions would see this prayer as a psychoneurotic betrayal of Christianity where sinusoidal feelings of deep insecurity have inseminated their customary defensive technique of radical articulations to obtain noticeability and to soothe the pain of the unnoticed child, or as a fervid philosophical predisposition where a sedulous application of Ockham's razor[1] has so denuded the notion of explanation that only the banalities of austere appearances survive. But I suppose many, if not most, within the church will, if not must, without a whisper of hesitancy but with a predatory inflexibility, interpret this petition as a psychological accommodation to placate an exceedingly postmodern conscience where atheistic predilections have lodged and metastasized within the soul's interior chambers, where inherent and cultivated affections for truth, belief, tradition, certainty, and ultimacy have all but evaporated within the advance of faithlessness. Other Christians who possess a more precise theological pathology will mark this prayer as the carnal logic of an apostate mind where divine dichotomies of love and wrath, grace and law, and good and evil have dissolved into meaningless oppositions, and where divine holiness, majesty, and honor, in all of their

---

1 William of Ockham, a late thirteenth-century and early fourteenth-century English philosopher, scholastic, and friar, preferred simplicity over plurality when explaining a phenomenon, such that no assumptions or inferences should be made beyond those absolutely necessary to save the phenomenon's appearance.

radiant glory, have become nothing more than the vermicular movements of a dead superstition. I remain undeterred. Without a doubt, humility is needed on my part, but I will let these words take me where my heart has longed to go. I want to see your character for myself.

Even as Job, while at the axial point in his spiritual life, encumbered with profound perplexity and contradiction of why you, whom he believed to be infinitely fair, would cripple an upright man with unspeakable affliction and suffering, sought an explanation from you, I too, unashamed but not hardened and unafraid but not arrogant, seek a hearing with the creator. Even no callous and conceited soul should be considered as an eternal obstruction to a God utterly apathetic to the worst of human disposition. Unlike human apathy—a lethal unresponsiveness or detachment—your kind of *apatheia* is a beautiful passionate move that creates, surrounds, penetrates, and assumes our existence out of indestructible love that eclipses our cold indifference as though it were nothing at all. But not an eclipse that leaves us behind in our pathetic passivity, but an eclipse that transfigures our very being into a defectless, dynamic reflection of yourself, a flawless cadence of the divine heartbeat. Neither the metaphoric imagery of the potter and the clay nor the Apostle Paul's authoritarian interdiction against his hypothetical interlocutors who raised legitimate questions concerning your inscrutable architecture of human affairs is of any impediment to me.²

As with Job, question me, Lord, and I will answer you. Where was I when you laid the earth's foundation?³ I was in your heart. I am still there. It is because of this indissoluble connection that I desire to understand you for myself.

As you know, I come with no pretense of intellectual objectivity or penetrating perspicacity. Moreover, I have had no adornments of rapturous spiritual encounters. I have been shaped largely by my own choices and by the uncontrollable forces of nature, culture, people, and the plasticity of neural chemistry, along with the innumerable gradations and constant flux of human experience. My approach to you is simplistic, and my questions are tolerable and reasonable.

Two thousand years ago, the cross changed the course of history, and its effects remain powerfully present in

---

2 Romans 9:19–33. I am inclined to think that the Apostle's somewhat abrupt answers to his imaginary inquisitive characters arose out of the natural liberty we tend to take and sometimes pervert for those we deeply love—in Paul's case, the Jewish people—so that the crucial catalyst for his caustic prescription was really love, not theology.

3 Job 38:3–4.

every continent, community, church, and Christian home. At first only a few pedestrian and otherwise unremarkable men took notice. And yet, the cross has made an epochal claim on our reality, one fundamentally different from other historical developments like tools, agriculture, and social organization. This is because we must interpret the cross when we confront it. Each person who engages the cross must ask, "What does the death of your son mean?"

I realize, Father, that the basic meaning of the cross originates with the apostles and must have taken form and been crystalized by their post-resurrectional experience. This makes perfect sense. If a friend of mine, who I thought might change the world, dies and then returns fully alive to share some fish cooked over an open fire on a beach, then the meaning of his death becomes an inescapable question to me.[4] I must understand why. The nature of this quest for early Christians surely became more imperative when the young church began to recognize that the one who died on the cross was as divine as you are, that he was in truth your only son.

To explain the divine reason for Jesus's death, theology has advanced three theories or themes of the cross

---

4 John 21:1–14.

over the course of history: substitutionary atonement, victorious subjugation, and moral exemplarity.[5] These themes are not so much distinct from each other as they are complementary. They share common elements to account for the work of Christ on the cross. Each is a generative framework that helps us to interpret the nature of Christ's work as a person, from his divine conception, virgin birth, sinless life, and innocent death, while looking beyond the cross to see the resurrection, life of the church, and finality, all of which comprise your reconciliation of us to yourself.

I think Karl Barth's phrase "God against us and God for us" apprehends the texture of substitutionary atonement. As the theme goes, there is no opposition as massive or monstrous as the one poised between you, a holy God, and sinful man. The enormity of this hostile aversion is an unfathomable repulsion beyond the greatest of human comprehension. The purity and strength of divine holiness, also immeasurable, can face neither this antinomic state nor the sinful creatures that created it. Divine wrath and judgment, therefore, are unavoidable necessities. Not even your holy love may eliminate the

---

5 Some theologians prefer to use the word "theme" or "motif" because "theory" contains a bit too much hypothesizing or speculation, and not enough facticity and certainty.

holy inevitability. Judgment necessitates punishment, an eternally irreversible retribution required by the very nature of goodness—your character. Evil has no lasting abode within your universes. Holiness demands evil's total eradication, and unfortunately for humanity, which hosts the parasitic corruption, holiness demands infinite punishment for our evil.

There's more. According to the theme, you also require restitution, an atonement for each evil thought we have had or deed we have committed, whether deliberate or accidental, isolated or habitual. Every transgression must be offset by reparation. You cannot simply ignore sin. You cannot look the other way because there's no other way for you to look. Your holiness and judgment are forever irremissible. This is the "God against us."

But, as the theme holds, "thanks be to God," for you have taken the judgment upon yourself and made restitution for all through the cross of Christ. Your perfect, only son willingly and lovingly stepped out of eternity and into time, took the form of a humble servant, laid his spent earthly life on the cross, shed his blood, absorbed an endless ocean of divine wrath, extinguished raging rivers of human guilt, paid a mountainous penalty, and permanently atoned for the sin of the world. With these divine and human acts of vicarious sacrifice and substitution, your judgment, mercy, and forgiveness stood victorious and rejoicing. But more significantly, the crucifixion was the event where you, in the fullness of Trinitarian power, infinity, eminence, holiness, glory, and life, hung in our place and on our behalf in weakness, temporality, humility, accusation, shame, and death, and overcame the reign of sin. This is the "God for us."

For the theme of victorious subjugation, the personification of evil in the form of Satan becomes the arrestive point of defeat through the crucifixion and resurrection. The theme implies that the world is too wicked for humanity to be the source of evil. The root of evil must reside in a being more formidable than man. Its eradication, therefore, must require divine measures beyond our tenuous abilities. It is a battle between heavenly beings fought within the venue of earthly beings where the ultimate destiny of man was at stake and where the father of lies, sin, and death had invaded creation. But the victorious cross and resurrection had destroyed the source of all sin and each of its integrals and derivatives. The calculus of sheer evil had been subdued and shattered. On that account, the opportunity for humanity to be liberated from the bondage of the echoes of a conquered but still living principality of darkness had been procured, but with a payment to Satan himself. The Gospel of Mark has

Jesus saying that "For even the Son of Man did not come to be served, but to serve, and to give his life as a ransom for many."[6]

Over the centuries, the victory of Christ theme seems to have wavered in its appeal and popularity. At the crest of the wave, early Christianity saw evil as demonic powers embodied within the devil, whose dethroning was the only way to defeat those powers. The cross represented an almost monetary transaction where you paid Satan off with the sacrifice of your son in exchange for Satan's relinquishment of his serpentine forces. The imagery and method of Christ's victory became more sophisticated as the cross was seen by some Christians like a duplicitous pretext designed to trick Satan into exceeding his authority and control over humanity by engaging the perfection of Christ on the cross. With the human nature of Jesus as the bait and his divine nature as the hook, the devil had been caught.

At the trough of the wave where the rationality of man had taken center stage, the popularity of the devil and this creative imagery began to dissipate, as they were perceived to be superstitious nonsense. The theme later reawakened when the brutality of man and his inner darkness became

---

6 Mark 10:45.

so globally and acutely visible that the promise of human reason began to relent. Putting aside the dynamics of this history, the heart of victorious subjugation is the idea that the crucifixion was necessary for the ascendancy of Christ over the dominion of evil, whether evil was viewed more traditionally as incarnate iniquity or more modernly as inauthentic existence.

The theme that the cross should be understood as an example of the highest morality, a selfless, sacrificial practice of life with a principled goodness directing every move and a relentless, unconditional obedience, without regard to where it may lead, even death, is one of individual subjectivity. Conceptualizing the crucifixion in this way provides an invocation and inspiration for us to love as you love and to give as you gave up the life of your son.

To see with the eyes of the soul the broken, bloody, and breathless Christ as he hung nailed to a cross is to see an exquisite exposition of your love for humanity. It is also a glimpse of humanity's own fractures, wounds, and convulsions that each person faces when choosing between a love for you and others and a love only for themselves. We must decide either to entomb our love within the secretions of selfishness or to spend it for you and creation until there's nothing left, just as Christ spent his love for you and your offspring until the darkness of death had overcome, but only to be resurrected for an endless divestiture of love for all things made through Christ our God. This is the poignancy of the exemplary theme of the cross. Christians, too, must take up their cross and follow Christ. The theme also neutralizes some of the juridical overtones of substitutionary atonement.

All of these themes, which have shaped Christian thought and practice for nearly two thousand years, have changed throughout different historical contexts. But, while superstition yields to rationalism, tradition yields to liberalism, and exclusivity yields to pluralism, the defining contours of each theme have remained essentially the same. Your immutable character endures. To see that character displayed in the cross of your son, to understand it, is my beginning, my passion, and my obsession.

This is quite an inelegant explanation of why the traditional narratives of the cross have maintained an inescapable core of violent necessity throughout ages of historical displacements and transitions. Simple and complex forces must have been at work. The sheer influence of Scripture has surely contributed to the durability of the cross. Maybe the affinity we have for a story where absolute good conquers absolute evil played a role. Perhaps our abhorrence of purposeless events, especially vastly consequential ones such as the cross, has been a factor. The horror of the cross is so great that you must have been at work through your dead son who hung on it to achieve something of comparable magnitude.

But doubt never sleeps and questions always stir, even when faced with two millennia of ecclesiastical tradition that Christ's death on the cross secured the promise of beatific immortality for those who believe. Disquietude lurks beneath that enduring tradition, a disquietude that I believe comes from you. We should see this as a calm hesitation, not as an anxious one, because your character will not and cannot allow a person's flawed beliefs or lack of any beliefs at all to ultimately derail the eternal fulfillment of the indestructible bond between the divine and the human. No one is going to hell because they hold unorthodox views. This sort of sounds like it doesn't matter what a person thinks about you or thinks you do not exist. No. What matters is that for something to really matter to a person does not require some other person, for whom that something may not matter, to suffer.[7]

---

[7] For a scriptural predicate for this assertion, see the parable of the vineyard laborers in Matthew 20:1–16.

CHAPTER 2

The Inquisition

My fundamental question is this: Did you require the crucifixion of your son to atone for a fallen humanity? This inquiry, really the heart and soul of this prayer, concerns not so much your method as your character; because the former, although not as separate and distinct from the latter in any synthetic sense, must be eternally consistent with your character, one and the same in a single and inexhaustible infinite act, with no division or deviation. Many versions of this basic question abound in countless nuances, indicating at once your nature, your attributes, and the benefits you confer—the God you are.

Was the passion of Christ, his pain, suffering, and death, indispensable to the salvation of humanity, or even to the redemption of the universe? Was the provision of an executed criminal an obligatory revelation of your nature, a "criminal" in whom abided a perfected humanity, a consummate and exquisite reflection of all that is divine, expressed in every thought, word, or deed, every encounter, every endeavor, every moment of silence or service, and every denial, rejection, or hatred? Does the creed of your holiness, majesty, and honor demand an immeasurable sacrifice of an immeasurable life? Are torture and asphyxiation necessary events within the divine economy? Was a violent, bloody death an unwaivable condition to your mercy, a nonnegotiable condition that had to be fully satisfied? Is the Godhead, from whom flows with perfect reciprocity an inconceivable intensity of love, joy, fellowship, and feasting, horrified by a deformed and contemptuous humanity?

Does my depravity—regardless of its depth, scope, magnitude, fervency, or repulsiveness—make the slightest indentation in your character? When your dignity or esteem is deliberately or unintentionally encroached upon by the spawn of your love, do you require an infinite restitution? Does a single act of evil jeopardize your Trinitarian harmony? Is a single divine act of pardon without punishment, forgiveness without suffering, or mercy without pain an eternal impossibility? Would it weaken or threaten the boundary between good and evil? Would cosmic law and order collapse if you remitted one sin without shedding blood?

Do your justice and mercy clash without pause when sin is born and until a pleasing substitution is made—the innocent for the guilty, the immaculate for the reprobate, the unblemished for the stained, the honorable for the abominable? Does the presentation of your son on the cross subdue that inner conflict? Does your enormous wrath gloriously subside and ultimately disappear by the anguish of Christ, or does your prodigious anger anesthetize and vanish when the blood of your only begotten son exudes and radiates from his head, his hands, his side, and his feet? Is this how you so loved the world?

Do human reasonableness, rationality, and conscience arise from you, or are they transitory vehicles of human origin, the earthly operating principles to subdue the conflict between chaos and order? My God, my God, are you reasonable? Are you rational? Do you have a conscience? Do these realities operate within your immanence? If they come from you, then why do the church's explanations of the crucifixion offend our rational faculties? Why do they sear our consciences?

Is sin so powerful and persuasive that it penetrates Trinitarian immunity? Or is iniquity solely an earthly and angelic problem that can only be eradicated by the death of a perfect human—Jesus himself? If sin is no match for your transcendence, and only efficacious within the realm of creation, then why must your methods with us be fundamentally different from your methods with your son and spirit? What is it about evil that requires or permits you to act in a way on earth that is inconsistent with how you have always acted in heaven? Do the sin borne and suffering endured by Christ accomplish a victory that you were otherwise unable to accomplish? Did they give you a freedom within human affairs that you did not always already possess? Do the dark forces of evil mandate the crucifixion in order to overthrow and annihilate them—as though they were spiritual black holes with those metaphorical naked singularities that swallow up the light of life and even life itself as they move across the universe of humanity?

Did the cross rectify a deficiency within the Godhead, did it fill a vacancy, did it strengthen your love, did it enlarge your mercy, did it augment your character or virtue? Did you rejoice on behalf of heaven and earth as you watched the misery of your only son while he hung gruesomely on the cross? Does violence make you feel good?

Is the death of Christ solely a paradigmatic model that we must imitate? Was the road from Gethsemane to Golgotha intended as a pattern for us to follow? Through the cross were you trying to show us your son's elaborate interiority, his tireless submissiveness, his vigorous willpower, his unrelenting loyalty to you, and his deep emotional integrity underneath feelings of fear, doubt, estrangement, and loneliness? Does the fact that Christ lovingly and joyfully consented to his crucifixion, and from the beginning, before the foundation of the world was laid, obeyed the divine instruction without coercion and willingly offered himself up to you, justify the act of violence?

As for your justice, how does punishment negate a sinful act or condition? If retribution serves no amendatory purpose, has no reformative quality, or results in a glacial indifference about a rehabilitation or newness of life for humanity, then is punishment only sheer vengefulness, precipitous hostility, and embittered vindictiveness? Would not your wrath be simply wrath, without possessing any remedial goal, having no purifying objective, and untouched by any invigorating content? And if that were the case, would not your love and wrath stand in perpetual confrontation? Or is your wrath a divine expedient to safeguard your holiness? Is it a shield to insulate your majesty from the sinfulness of your creatures?

What is this two-thousand-year-old theological discourse about a staggering debt incurred or a scandalous price that was paid for our sin? Is this not punishment expressed in economical terms? Isn't this a monetary exchange designed to justify the ignition of eternal flames? Was this the ransom that Jesus paid? Was this the debt he assumed? Did his pain and suffering really discharge our debt?

Having offered these questions, I will not refuse to inquire into these matters, nor will I accept with tranquil equanimity that your divine decrees or whatever you permit, though often mysterious and cloaked with inarticulate purpose and meaning, are enough for me, or are a sufficient explanation for which no further inquiry is allowed. I perpetually recall from one of your greatest visionaries the admonition of caution that "it is with the holiest fear that we should approach the terrible fact of the sufferings of our Lord."[1] But I will not yield to these intellectually impermeable paradoxes, concede before these unfathomable divine anomalies, bow to these ecclesiastically sacred imponderables, move into a theological state of mental intermission, and take refuge within a seemingly destitute assurance that all will be well with my soul if I believe in the orthodox explanations of your atoning sacrifice, if

---

[1] George MacDonald, *Unspoken Sermons: Series I* (Whitethorn: Johannesen, 1999), 110.

I endorse the salvific transactions consummated on the cross, or if I trust that the death of your only son paid my infinite debt and pardoned my soul. What does faith require: that we ignore the questions the cross presents, or that we accept your invitation to explore them?

We should not retreat to the old sanctuary of substitutionary atonement or to the fortress of a victorious crucifixion or to the ivory tower of an indefectible example because these theories reveal nothing of your true character. Instead, they disfigure it beyond the recognition of anything good. Torture and torment, either of your creatures or of Christ, do not satisfy you. They do not cover sin, but create it. They do not advance justice, but destroy it. They do not protect your holiness, but attack it. They do not reveal your divine sovereignty, but humanize it.

Suffering may have a role within a pagan god of human imagination, but it has no place within the God you are. Your goodness is what makes you beautiful and your fairness is what makes your beauty so realizable by a humanity severed from our true selves. Fairness is not a divine quality that arose because of our sin. Fairness is an eternal quality that has always been shared among the persons of the Trinity. There it is unconditional and free. Fairness *is* because of who you are. The birth of evil did not alter it. Fairness remains the same because you do.

You are reasonable. No reasonable human being would spill the blood of the innocent to forgive the guilty, to conquer evil, or to set an example for all to follow—and we are only finitely reasonable. You are infinitely reasonable. It's impossible for our reasonableness to exceed yours. But the theologies of the cross deface your reasonableness. When these explanations are done, all that remains of your face for the human mind to behold is an ugly incoherency, a poor, mean, and inconsequential God worthy of worship from only the faithless. It's as though the actual monitorial of the early apostles was, "Let no one beguile you, not of the simplicity that is in Christ Jesus, but of his unreasonableness."[2]

There's no story that captures the spirit of true belief for me more than when Saint Wulfram attempted to baptize the Frisian Radbod in the eighth century. Although the story is likely apocryphal, it is potent. Legend has it that when Saint Wulfram promised Radbod the destination of heaven if only he would step into the baptistry, Radbod asked about the destination of his ancestors. When he heard that they lived in hell, Radbod refused baptism. That's faith. He preferred an eternal hell with his family instead of an eternal heaven without them. He rejected a

---

2   2 Corinthians 11:3.

capricious God who required a simple profession of faith with a simple ceremonial procedure as the doorway to life eternal, and doomed those who had not performed this rite to an endless life of abandonment and misery.

We must see you in the cross of Christ with the same fearlessness. We must let go of our unbeliefs that swallow your goodness beneath a sea of explanations and begin to believe the God you are in truth. What better way to begin than to understand that you did not create us to live on a knife's edge where the content of our theology or the absence of any theology at all determines on which side of the eternal blade we end up, all the while being shredded by your love.

CHAPTER 3

The Unbelief

I have never doubted the crucifixion of Christ as a historical event. But the tireless perpetuation of its traditional meanings and significance are only toxic intorsions, all tightly wrapped around the axis of unbelief, and with pendulous tentacles of distrust, denial, and repudiation, each revealing not the truth of your character but the utter perversion of it. Those abominable theological explanations belittle you, reduce you to the point where belief becomes possible. They are as dishonorable of who you are as they are disrespectful of how you move, as bankrupt of divine content as they are solvent with incredulity, as immune to your thoughts as they are darkened of your ways. Those explanations have an imperceptible vision, an ugly aesthetic, and a legalistic belief. They have seized and paralyzed our hearts and minds from engaging the inspiration and power of your goodness. They have infected us with the fantasy of axiomatic words like "propitiation," "exoneration," "adoption," "justification," and "imputation"—words appropriate for a God who is thought so little of. They have created mountainous obstructions to your simplicity by distorting your true nature. They have relieved us, not of the crushing impossibilities of your demands, which are imaginary, but of our true and only destiny—sharing in your life and love with every contingent thread of our being.

Even the berating of Celsus[1] and the piercing insight of Nietzsche, perhaps your greatest atheists, are inferior inflictions, if not only minor irritants, compared to those nauseating theories of atonement offered by the church, especially substitutionary atonement, including its most impoverished forms. In truth, atheistic views cannot rival our evil innovations to explain the cross's necessity. The godless caricature of Christians as croaking frogs on the shores of shallow ponds, the declaration that God is dead, or the assertion that Christianity has displaced the essence of all that is truly good in humanity—the power of

---

[1] Celsus was an opponent of Christianity during the second century.

determination—with the essence of all that is truly bad—the poverty of weakness—are mere flea bites when compared to the Christian belief that a violent crucifixion is the divine catalyst for mercy, forgiveness, and healing. It is better to believe that "God is dead" than it is to believe in a God who designed depraved deformities of atonement. To willfully misconceive you is a graver sin than to deny you. At least in denial we might apprehend the truth of your character, but in misconceiving you we do far more violence to the apprehension of your beauty.

We are saturated with unbelief. We refuse to accept that it is simply your nature to forgive, that it is as much within your power to remit the sin as it is to love the sinner, and that your infinite mercy within your infinite being requires no internal or external fulfillment of any condition, no juridical preparation or arrangement for the outpouring of your pardon, no deferment of reprieve until your wrath abates, and no satisfaction of your justice before our souls receive the gift of absolution. You forgave us when we were not, just as you loved us when we were not. But yet with an impressive recalcitrance, as intense as it is relentless, which is a derivative of your love but misappropriated by us to further entrench our misguided intellects, these unbelieving spirits of ours fanatically insist that you cannot be at liberty to simply forgive. We will not understand that you are capable of being merciful without a cost, or some sort of curtailment of your character, and that your forgiveness can come without punishment, pain, and suffering. Before we can believe, we must abridge your freedom, dilute the truth of your being, and confine your mercy within the parochial boundaries of our flaccid faith.

It seems strange that Christians thunder away about your unconditional love, extol its inexhaustibility, praise its paradoxical nature, and ceremonialize its meritlessness. But when it comes to your mercy, they launch explanatory expeditions into its complexity, its conditionality, and its incompatibility with your justice. It's as though they envision your love, justice, and mercy as points of an equilateral triangle within which confrontation and conflict rage before and after the foundations of the earth were laid, until the cross of Jesus Christ either harmonizes the vertices of repulsion into a Hegelian synthesis[2] of some grander system or arbitrates an acceptable compromise so that each may yield some ground to the others, but ultimately retain its mysterious enmity for them.

Even some theologians have ludicrously suggested that

---

2   A reference to Georg Wilhelm Friedrich Hegel, a nineteenth-century German philosopher who believed that knowledge was obtained through a dynamic synthesis of contradiction and negation.

sin actually presented an almost unsolvable dilemma for you. They believed, or more accurately, having disguised authentic unbelief as authentic belief, that the unthinkable antagonism among your love, justice, and mercy caused by our iniquitous condition introduced within the Trinity a predicament so severe that it barely hovered above the horizon of divine impossibility, and could only be resolved by an act equally severe—the crucifixion of Christ.[3]

You are bound by neither time nor events. You are not determined by them. They do not constrain you. They do not change you. This means, among other glorious things, that the dawn of sin within the human heart did not alter the state of your heart from what that state would have been had there been no sin. The perception that we all stand before you with the pulverizing burden of a non-dischargeable debt, which only the criminal death of the innocent can relieve, is miserably mistaken.

Rather than believe in the God you are, many Christians invent a God that you're not. This invention is a more harmful form of idolatry because, rather than exalting a lifeless object, it defames your character. In doing so, they disavow your simplicity; they deny the strength and

---

[3] A good example of this is the book by John R. W. Stott, *The Cross of Christ* (Downers Grove: InterVarsity Press, 1986).

goodness of your love; they criminalize your righteousness. With substitutionary atonement, you must kill to forgive, punish to absolve, disburse wrath upon the innocent to acquit, and act unjustly to restore your justice. Because Christians have been so poisoned by the noxious fumes of substitutionary atonement, because they have been gripped by unspeakable fear that their souls may be in danger if their thinking deviates from the traditional understanding of the sacred texts, and because they refuse to consider whether there is anything at all about you not found in the Bible worthy of contemplation, they cannot see, seek, or find the truth of your character. They are unable to perceive your love, justice, and mercy, not as entangled within a web of opposing forces, but as supplementing each other in an incandescent indivisibility that creates, pardons, renews, and enfolds the creature within the uninterruptable life of joy, peace, and communion that the Trinity shares within itself in a timeless consummate exchange. This is your nature; the lifeless machinery of doctrinal black boxes does not exist within you.

Christianity paints a picture of the human condition that looks like a financial statement, with all of our debts to be paid and restitutions to be made. But we are unable to perform up to your divine standard according to basic Christian doctrine. We have no spiritual assets from which to discharge our liabilities, nothing of intangible value to satisfy our obligations of redress. So what's the salvific narrative offered by Christianity for such spiritual destitution? A story that sounds more like a synthesis of Aristophanic and Shakespearean comedies than one containing the powerful and poignant drama of a God whose love and commonsense rule unabated by our condition.[4] We're implored to attend the theological Thinkery—that is, the church—to learn the new way of escaping our debt-laden past, because you are intoxicatingly bound to extract your "pound of flesh" to satisfy your insatiable appetite for justice.

This simply is not you as seen in Christ. Whatever atonement we're required to make, to you as well as to others, we and we alone must make it. We have an eternity within which to do so; we have an endless supply of your grace, strength, courage, justice, and love to amend our selfishness, injustices, wrongs, and hatefulness. That your son must satisfy our debts by death is a fabrication, an artifact of fortified unbelief. It reflects our desire for a duplicitous deliverance.

---

[4] In Aristophanes's *The Clouds*, Philippides was encouraged by his father to attend Socrates's Thinkery to learn the art of rhetoric to weasel out of his debts. In Shakespeare's *The Merchant of Venice*, Shylock was obsessed with the desire to "extract his pound of flesh" from his debtor.

By a kind of Kierkegaardian irrationality[5] we actually believe that punishment cancels sin, pain neutralizes evil, and that suffering eradicates the offense. As we are so neurotically obsessed with the consequences of wicked deeds and thoughts, our irrationality ascends further up to the summit of psychopathic theology. It is there, the state of absolute religious insanity, that abstract suffering fails to gratify us. We demand more. We require the punishment of the sinless and the suffering of the holy.

And as though that were not enough, we have been admonished by Martin Luther to engage in perpetual, self-induced prostrations before a mental image of Christ on the cross and employ the tormenting tactics of emotional laceration, impalement, and disintegration as the only appropriate Christian approach to the crucifixion.[6] If *Macbeth* had been written a few decades earlier, Luther could have used Lady Macbeth as the exemplary psychological state to which we all must strive as we contemplate the cross—that long and lonely descent into guilt, horror, and madness, unconsciously crying, "Yet here's a

---

5   A reference to Soren Kierkegaard, a nineteenth-century Danish philosopher who believed that authentic faith was essentially irrational.
6   Martin Luther, "A Meditation on Christ's Passion" (1519). Reprinted in Timothy F. Lull, *Martin Luther's Basic Theological Writings* (Minneapolis: Fortress Press, 1989), 165–172.

spot . . . Out, damned spot! Out, I say!" as we uselessly wash our hands to remove the irremovable stains of your son's blood because of our sin. Luther was perhaps your most compelling sixteenth-century reformer in terms of the energy of his will, the richness of his passion, and the clarity of his thought, although his energetic will was laced with profound irony, his passion ultimately died under the weight of his despotic doctrine, and his clear thought was no guarantee of accuracy. Unbelief was the cornerstone of much of his teaching.

Suffering has always held a predominant role in the Christian narrative, and it has served an indispensable function in understanding the crucifixion. I dissent from this role and function. Suffering may be an inalienable part of the human condition, but it is not intrinsically holy. It has no divine quality or meaning. Suffering is vacuous and inessential. It conquers nothing. It does not teach anything that cannot be taught in a more favorable environment. It does not enlighten anyone who cannot be enlightened without pain. We were not made for suffering. We were made for goodness.

Have I gone too far with these sentiments, oh God? Many people have claimed that moral reinforcement, spiritual strengthening, or other beneficial qualities were occasioned by their personal suffering. Some believe that there's no better way to see your sovereignty displayed than when you bring them within an inch of their lives by divine decree. Well, I have no desire here to speak about the best pastoral practices to serve those who suffer, and I have no satisfactory answer to the question of why there's so much suffering in this world you made. Nor am I making any advancement of the insolvent idea that material prosperity is reserved for those who believe that leisure and luxury are your end game. I wish to expose, for the benefit of the believer, the flawed theological link between sin and pain, between atonement and suffering.

Not one single sin, mortal or venial, that has ever been committed is negated by suffering. Christians claim that the pain of Christ offsets sin and that his suffering is necessary for salvation. But why? They believe that you required a divine synthesis of a unique pain, suffering, death, and a unique person—that is, the pain, suffering, and death of the perfectly holy one by the most excruciating method—the Roman crucifixion. So, I suppose that if Christ had been plagued with chronic pain, such as headaches, lower-back pain, or arthritic conditions, followed by death, or if he had died as a toddler after a long bout with leukemia, those life and death experiences would have been unsatisfactory to secure an atonement for a bunch of worthless creatures. The sinfulness of humanity is too great for those pedestrian experiences of pain and death to be of any divine value.

Christians insist that you needed your son's abrupt, acute, and debilitating pain. They say that you required his devastating bodily injury, loss of blood, and the despondency and despair of being forsaken by you, his disciples, and his people, and all this torment followed by a glacial death through suffocation! You needed to recapitulate thousands of years of animal sacrifice with all the nuanced symbolism of blood, unbroken bones, and spotlessness in one superlative sacrifice for the sin of the world. Christians would support their belief with the argument that because of the perfect humanity of your incarnate son, his suffering and death transcended the physical realm and moved into the spiritual realm, where he suffered with a greater intensity than could ever be felt by a depraved human, all enveloped by a dark, nebulous intercourse within the Godhead, beyond the reach of our exiguous intellects.

Those sedimentary assertions have clearly settled in the basement of a hollow intellectual integrity. Whether suffering is physical or spiritual, mild or intense, disclosed or hidden, suffering is suffering. To characterize the suffering of Christ as the divine epitome of centuries of temple sacrificial practice does not dignify his suffering. It's only another mournful explanation to infuse meaning where it doesn't belong. The cross neither anticipates nor establishes an economy of suffering through which you can interact with the world. If it had, then violence would be the sole medium for your goodness between heaven and earth.

To also argue that the consent of Christ to the death march from Gethsemane to Golgotha mysteriously transforms this lunacy into saneness, not only misses the point, but is itself a superficial distraction, and completely fails to mitigate the absurdity. To the contrary, this argument magnifies it. The acquiescence of Christ to his own barbaric and merciless death at your hands as his Father only serves to make your son complicit in the murderous divine arrangement.

Some Christians may say that there's an important moral distinction here that should not be overlooked, and one that even Christ himself made clear—"No one takes [my life] from me, but I lay it down of my own accord."[7]

---

[7] John 10:18. A related but more memorable saying of Jesus is: "Greater love has no one than this, that he lay down his life for his friends." John 15:13. Who would not be moved by this quality of love, a superlative selflessness having no regard for personal vulnerability? Selfless exposure to risk may be an important and necessary element of love shared among a world of broken beings, but it's only the invulnerable love of God that can restore broken beings. There's no such thing as risk within the Godhead.

They believe that the strength of his mind and mastery, as reflected in the Gospel of John's version of the Passover discourse between the Lord and his disciples, establishes the divine necessity of the cross. But the essence of my prayer is that violence is not a part of your character. It has no role to play within the Trinitarian life and love shared among the Godhead. Whether Christ is seen as a casualty or champion of the cross, or whether he acquiesces or dissents to his death, is of no consequence. Christians have been led astray by these deceptive irrelevancies. A prophet of yours once decried that "the heart is deceitful above all things and beyond cure. Who can understand it?"[8] No truer words could be spoken when the heart of the believer, with exquisite deception, constructs such preposterous theories of atonement.

This sentiment is especially the case when the amplitude of suffering crosses a critical threshold that calls the durability of a person's mental and emotional life into question or vitiates a person's ability to process the pain and accommodate the cataclysmic change. That the degree of suffering is correlated with the degree of redemption is itself a cruelty. The reality of suffering is not redeemable.

Take, for example, a child's death. It crushes that

---

8 Jeremiah 17:9.

threshold for parents. The physical and emotional void left by the final absence of a child shatters the psychological integrity and stability of the mother and father, not to say anything of the depredatory effects on other siblings. The face, eyes, smile, laugh, tears, touch, voice, the entire personality and presence of the child have ended, permanently withdrawn from the loving embrace of the parents where the only reality remaining is held within the heart of their memory. The toil of that experience is hopelessly beyond difficult and approaches ineffability. When the suffering Christian considers that Christ, your very son, was not immune from human travesty but joyfully embraced it, the believer may think that you have somehow sanitized personal suffering, that the cross was the unparalleled vindication of human pain, or worse, that the cross was the place where you claimed the redeemable qualities of violence. It is a cruelty all its own that something so world shattering as the death of a child is held to be redeemable. To hold this doctrine negates both the uniqueness of the child and the degree of suffering. It sees the child's death as a pretext for something greater. In doing so, it sees you as a divine being who exercises his will on the back of unimaginable suffering.

These pathways of thought attempt to find explanation and comfort for our sorrow, but they are destructive to our understanding of you. They shrink your goodness to make room for our pain. They envenomate your character to reconcile our grief. They replace your peace with turbulence. When the dust settles on these perilous reflections, we're left with a bloodthirsty God, not as a clamorous spectator, but as a reposeful architect whose radical stimulus for mercy is suffering. The violent cross redeemed violence by erasing our sin, easing your anger, and executing your judgment. Oh God, how far have we fallen to believe this of you?

Ultimately, whatever comfort a person finds in the suffering of Christ seems fleeting, a consolation that fades with the passage of time. The crucified Christ may be a companion in pain, perhaps the ultimate one, but any derivative comfort has no lasting healing effect. The shock and sting of a tragic event may slowly abate and the intensity of the hurt may weaken, but the sufferings of our Lord neither redeem nor renew.

Is not the latent prayer of any suffering believer not only the elimination of pain but also the return of love lost, the recovery of life perished, and the restoration of joy departed? The love, life, and joy of God, not a God who suffers, are the hope of our redemption. Those are the qualities eternally possessed by and shared among the Trinitarian persons. Suffering has no province or pursuit within your relations. Who would not want to share in your unfading immunity to suffering, to enjoy your magnanimous beauty when all that was lost, but is worth saving, will be fully renewed forever? In the meantime, we do not need to tyrannize ourselves with the burden of accommodating suffering or to baptize our afflictions and call them holy. Rather, we should condemn them because you will eliminate them.

For many, the crucifixion of Christ validates the worth of humanity in your holy eyes. It shows the lengths to which you went to save us. It proves that there are no obstacles to your love for us. Those convictions are best expressed in the Apostle Paul's profession: "He who did not spare his own son, but gave him up for us all . . . "[9]—a declaration as specious as it is consoling. It is bizarre, if not totally twisted, for Christians to measure the depth of their value to you or the intensity of your love for them by the strength of your unwillingness to refrain from crucifying your son. Every Sunday we worship you as if pain is an expression of divine love. Nietzsche was right. Christianity is addicted to brokenness, not only its own but also to Christ's. Suffering is seen not only as natural, but as a

---

[9] Romans 8:32.

duty we must embrace. Suffering is consecrated as a means of perfection and anointed as a path to virtue.

The benign desire for a companion in pain can also degenerate into a fundamentally broken belief that sees the cross as necessary for you to truly understand human sorrow, as though the crucifixion of your son filled a divine deficiency with a piece of painful human experience. That perception negates your omniscience prior to the cross, but affirms it after the cross. Violence becomes the concluding phase of the evolution of your knowledge. The same would be true of your love. Without the violence of the cross, your love would have remained incomplete.

Unfortunately, however, the degeneration doesn't stop there. It is only a disposition of decadence that sees the cross as an event which, in some sense, you deserved. This attitude sees the crucifixion as a sort of reverse reparation for having created a world with so much suffering. With this thinking, you assumed full responsibility for our defective, disintegrated, and destructive beings by sacrificing your only son. The death of Christ was your entrance into concrete solidarity with your creation. It's as though you did not foresee or anticipate an error in the order of creation. Your miscalculations have made you beholden to our delinquencies, an indebtedness that you alone must repay.

Of course, all of that is nonsense, and relies on an incoherent and demented doctrine about you. If you exist outside of time, then all of you must be timeless, with no part left to undergo some mutational process of deification. Indeed, if you created us without fully understanding us, then we're all in trouble. And if divine suffering is the corridor to a sacred coalition between the creator and the created, then you're a barbarian after all. The utterly absolute goodness of your being, upon which all of creation rests, is vulnerable to the fractures of sin that must be filled with feats of cruelty.

The same may be said of the idea of divine punishment because it too plumbs the depths of incoherency to draw up more sinister profanations about your character. Punishment does not annul or expunge a past sin. It removes nothing. It does not absolve prior evil acts. It neither offers any reversionary promise nor serves any other purpose. A person's repentance and atonement are the only things that can be done about an antecedent wrong. From the sinner's perspective and for the sinner's good, the effect of divine forgiveness lies in the amendatory dispositions and doings of the sinner and in no other place. I do not believe that you punish anyone for anything. Punishment is as far away from you as is the east from the west. You do not arrange secondary causes or appropriate natural tendencies within the universe to inflict punishment for punitive or disciplinary purposes. To believe that you are vindictive reflects an unweaned pubescency, an infant believer unfit for the solid food offered by the simplicity of your nature.

Punishment is exclusively provisional within the earthly realm and specifically operates within the relations of parent and child as well as civil authorities and citizens, serving only a corrective function. An "eye for an eye" theory of punishment may ease the retaliatory desire of a vengeful soul, but it has no purpose within the Godhead. Contrary to the scriptural proclamation, "vengeance" does not belong to you.[10] You do not claim possession of the idea, even if you know how to use it judiciously. With you there's no such thing as an eternal settling of the score.

It has been said over centuries that without your justice—the law of your being—our world would plunge into nihilistic anarchy, a moral entropy would permeate the human soul, and all order would slowly decompose and disperse until all that remained is a kind of thermodynamic equilibrium of rebellion. I believe this to be true. What I find untenable, however, is the church's understanding of the nature of your justice, its orientation, and

---

10 Deuteronomy 32:35.

how it works and unfolds in human experience. One word captures the nucleus of that understanding: punishment. It is an understanding of justice that either neglects love and mercy or sees justice, love, and mercy as competing divine forces where all three qualities have become disfigured on the field of battle within your mind. In either case, punishment is the victor.

There's no doubt that human rebellion—our defiance of you—must be removed, finally and fully. It can have no permanency or shadow of indestructibility within your creation. Not only may a faint drift of rebellion no longer dwell within our being, but your recapitulation of our self-definition and our character must be such that we no longer have the capacity to rebel. The question becomes whether your recapitulation must take the form of punishment. Are there alternatives? Yes, but even here one should be careful not to visualize you as a God who has multiple choices available to him to achieve his end and who lets his infinite wisdom guide him to make the best decision. I believe that how you are with us must be the same as how you are without us. The fact that you have a bunch of rebellious creatures who need to be reformed does not change you. I think, therefore, that you would not and could not punish us into submission. Your ways with us must correspond with your ways within the

Trinity. Although this is in no sense categorical, I see your manner with us as a delicate and intimate pursuit, a fair address and a peaceful persuasion, unconstrained by time, unobstructed by our sin, and unimpeded by our freedom.

Next to evil, punishment is a human reality furthest from you. You love us into existence and you love us into perfection. But assuming that the doctrine of substitutionary atonement is correct—that is, punishment is a divine necessity inasmuch as your justice mandates that it be carried out—then we must be punished, and no one else. To punish Christ in our place, to impute all of the world's sin to him, to hold him answerable to you for all of our iniquitous ways, is not justice but a cataclysmic injustice, an unthinkable reversal of all that is fair and good. To put one's faith in this revolting immorality—to believe that, given our paltry, fragile, and wretched nature, it was only Christ, in the form and substance of indefectible man, who could endure the tectonic power of your punishment—contradicts the very idea of a just God.

But this is of greater significance: When Christians engage that belief, they do not realize that they are categorically dismantling and abandoning the very thing they believe you require—punishment. According to Christians, if there's sin, there must be punishment, but the question of who should be punished for the sin is unimportant to them. So it's not punishment after all; it's only suffering. In effect, what Christians are actually saying about you is that if there's sin, then you demand the suffering of someone. For you to punish Christ on the cross would have had no curative purpose or remedial effect; he was innocent, perfect. To incarcerate your son within a prison of external and internal suffering all in the name of love, justice, and mercy is an act of the highest criminality. This theology achieves nothing other than to subvert the beauty of the divine infinite to the ugliness of divine masochism.

I feel that Christianity's initial intuitions about what you're like and what you demand of us are sound, but desecrated departures from soundness rapidly take root in the sidereal soils of the intellectual impulse to elaborate and justify. Christianity says that your justice requires the accountability of the sinner. I could not agree more. But to hold Christ accountable on the cross, to hold yourself accountable for our iniquity, is to unravel accountability altogether.

The idea of accountability that matters most to Christianity is eternal. Temporal accountability is of expendable value; it's unimportant in the grand scheme of the divine. Passing punishment can be conceded and endured. Eternal damnation is another matter entirely for Christians.

It is within this climactic context of either heaven or hell that the cross of Christ takes ultimate accountability off the table. Christ assumed final culpability and bore its damnatory sequel. Believers are free to go. With the divine magic of substitution, your wrath and justice were redirected toward yourself. Believers, now bathing themselves in your mercy and avoiding having to come as intolerable wretches face-to-face with your awful holiness that they have created, become answerable to no one.

In the church's doctrine of divine justice, Christians are set free. Whether the penalty and pain are too much for Christians to bear, or your wrath is too great for them to endure, or your holiness is too pure for them to live, their responsibility for evil does not exist in Christianity. It died with the death of your son. Why do Christians not see this as an outright exploitation of justice? A truthful answer is as unelaborate as your justice; the effortless sensibility of divine justice is too powerful for Christians to take. Their only refuge is contrived, mindless complexity that misconstrues and corrupts your goodness.

In its essence, your justice is fairness, a pure and infinite quality of decency, free of partiality and intolerance. Your justice discerns, forgives, corrects, and strengthens. It is a manifestation of your steadfast love, a love that loves with no withholding. The purpose of your justice in humanity is to make us just to each other, to make us fair in each encounter with our neighbor and to make us righteous, not with the selfish assertion of being right, but to be in love with all that is right and good. Our justice must be of a quality where we would recoil and tremble from one unjust thought, word, or deed toward another person. It must be full of openness, candor, charity, regard, deference, and on appropriate occasions determined by the wisdom of discernment, silence, an enlightened perspective—not with the sense of human apathy.

In addition to our perspective of your justice, as warped as it may be, divine wrath is another enduring delusion of the church, but with one pivotal saliency. Only an extant quality can be warped; a nonextant quality is a deceptive illusion, which may be more difficult to eradicate. I do recognize that we are constrained by language. And I suppose we do not desire a God with no emotional disturbances or dispirited affectivity. We're agitational creatures who expect our creator to be invigoratively responsive—delighted with our goodness and displeased with our badness.

Nevertheless, by institutional infliction, not from a Trinitarian source, we have been intoxicated with your wrath and tormented by your vexation. In the place above every place, you radiate holy anger, exhale a ferocious fury, and unleash the transitional storms of suffering and the eternal infernos of hell, all for those whom you first loved.[11] We have also been taught in the Scriptures that, in the early stages of humanity, you had become so enraged with our disobedience that you lamented having endowed the dust of the ground with your living breath, and then decided to bury the planet under a sea of water.[12] These few words, however, do not begin to capture the divine rampancy. "I will wipe mankind, whom I have created, from the face of the earth . . . "[13]

I will not dispute the fashionable explanation that our ancestry equated natural phenomena with the irritation of the gods, but I do think that such an explanation cannot account for the sustainability of Christianity's propensity for your anger. However, I wish to offer to you my view of Christianity's opening to the idea of divine wrath. As I write this part of my prayer early this morning, last night's energetic storms left behind a Petrine atmosphere, not of a crowing cock, but of a lumbering somber with its autograph of motionless and unelevated light-gray clouds with no transparency to anything remotely blue, accompanied

---

[11] 1 John 4:19.
[12] Genesis 6:5–7.
[13] Genesis 6:7.

by the routine aggravation of an intermittent and dull drizzle—a perfect setting for this morning's offering.

It seems to me that temple Judaism, Christianity's precursor, appropriated at least one pagan characteristic—the sacrificial extermination of something animated in the hope of subduing an inflamed divine disposition and extracting a more favorable one. This immolation was institutionalized shortly after the Red Sea experience and has continued for centuries. It was an erroneous appropriation. Because Christianity naturally incorporated some of the cultural features of its changing environment over the course of history, including paganism and Platonic philosophy, it should have taken a pagan-like lesson about the negligibility of doctrine—that unbending intellectual foundation on which to construct the intricacies of your character, a systematician's paradise where they may elucidate for us noviliates the nature of the divine being.

To pagans, doctrine was barely extant and played little, if any, role in their religious pursuits and practices. To Christianity, however, doctrine is crucial. It establishes a set of core beliefs about you, us, Christ, the church, and the end of time. It articulates the salient truths about the historical narrative of our salvation, from the incipient events within the Trinity before your initial utterances of creation; to the fall of humanity; the covenant with Israel;

the new covenant through Christ revealed in his birth, life, death, and resurrection; the church; and finally to your ultimate judgment, followed by unending treasure or torment. To say that Christian doctrine is a matter of life or death is a belittlement. It is a matter of eternal life or death. Diversity of ideas and interpretations may be permitted on the tassels of doctrine, but its infrastructural teaching must be not only believed but lived if one is to have a chance to be in your infinite presence. It is no wonder that institutionalized doctrine is so significant in the Christian hierarchy of values.

This exalted status is indefensible. It mocks your character. Human language can never fully and finally apprehend the truth of your nature, your idea of each of us, or your relationship to each of us, regardless of who speaks, including yourself. Language is diminutive by definition. Our articulated representations of you are always partial. But this inadequacy of language is an accessory to something more important. Not only can the truth of you in the fullness of the Trinity and the truth of us in the fullness of your mind not be systematized, they cannot be spoken at all. They cannot be explained. When a person attempts to do so, egocentricity, exclusivity, and errors quickly move in and the system becomes dictatorial. The theological skyscrapers of the past great systematicians impair more than clarify the relationship between you and us.

Parenthetically, I realize that when I pound away at one man's doctrine, I do so with my own hammer of dogmatics, an inescapable part of human nature. I prefer to visualize my sledgehammer as though I were Dante smashing to pieces the baptismal font to save a person from drowning as Dante recalls in "Canto XIX" of the *Inferno*—annihilation of sacred church doctrine to save a Christian from death.

Laying aside the scriptural argument, which I'll engage later in this prayer, if a Christian dare to examine the genuine reasons for their insistence on the necessity of your wrath, which is worthy of their reflection if they could break only for a few moments from their misguided adherence to biblical inerrancy, they may find at least two arguments—one psychological and the other theological. The psychotic need for your wrath is sort of an aggrandized and twisted sense of the believer's own significance. The higher the redemption price for their soul, the more their self-importance soars—a direct correlation between cost and value—almost an economically emotional assessment. This feeling is fundamentally different from the feeling of two apostles as they conversed about who should stand to the right and left of Christ in his kingdom.[14] The latter feeling is simple egotism; the former is far worse—a manipulative distortion of your character in order to elevate one's dignity, to enhance one's esteem, and to glorify one's importance. One feeling is a fairly benign preference to be seen rather than to see; the other is an egregious act of narcissism by deprecating your very nature as God. The "golden calves"[15] of our idolatry become more septic when they not only lie within as inert monuments of self-adoration, but when we inject them with animation and ambition.

The higher the feeling of our self-value ascends, the higher are our monotonous audibles about the death wage of sin and the more vociferous we become about our unworthy condition, sanctimoniously proclaiming our eternal death warrant. We think piety is achieved by the strength of devotion to our own fallen nature. For us, to magnify our utter worthlessness is to honor you. These errant thoughts propel divine wrath to higher and higher levels of theological prattle. Rather than believe in your simplicity, your eternal giving, and the unreserved abundance of your love, unimpeded by the most abysmal sin,

---

14 Mark 10:37.
15 Exodus 32:1–4.

the most ingrained rebellion, and the most unworthy sinner, the concave Christian curves further and further inward until theology is reduced to undiluted unbelief, eligible only for a God so absorbed by wrath that such a God must live by death, love by loss, and forgive by suffering.

The other reason for divine wrath is theological. Simply put, your wrath provides a foundational justification for the crucifixion of your son. The ecclesiastical fallacy progresses along the following lines: Your holiness is so infinitely pure and separate that you, the creator, cannot countenance an atomic particle of sin. You may not behold it, touch it, tolerate it, or live with it. Sin is forever antagonistic and repulsive to your holiness. It is this aversion in its transcendent amplitude that presumably represents for Christianity the core of your wrath—an anger so unimaginably intense that it required an unthinkable response. And the only way to express such a response that could be found within the depths of Trinitarian consciousness was a murderous cross. So, in the face of all that could be considered by any standard as uncivilized, unconscionable, and unintelligible, and against every charge of cruelty, sadism, and heartlessness (all of which the Christian will happily concede at every turn), your wrath demanded an answer as ungraspable as it is unyielding. All explanation ceases at that point. We are not permitted to trespass that boundary. Either we must accept that premise or we must die.

I do not believe in your wrath. As with punishment and pain, wrath has no residence within the Godhead; it has no place in the heart of the divine; it serves no purpose; it possesses no goodness; it has no originality or creativity; unlike love, wrath is reactionary; but like punishment, it works only in regression. Wrath is of our own making. It is part of our psychological interiority. It is subjectivity, highly effective but miserably inefficient. Wrath attacks and destroys. This is not to say that you have no power to destroy. You do destroy. But the one and only object of your destruction is sin, evil. No one, including Christ, was or will ever be the focus of your destructive power.

Some have said that wrath is the other side of your love. I suspect this too materialized from a desire to protect some semblance of an attribute of anger ascribed to you by the Scriptures and thousands of years of religious tradition. Nonetheless, that perspective also lies within the terrain of flawed human thought. Your love has no dimensions; it has no geometrical properties; it is not prismatic or reflective. The effects of your love, however, are chromatically diverse, a limitless spectrum of coloration and texture, an orchestrated synthesis of harmonic tones, movements, oscillations, and tempo. Your love is one infinite act without beginning, end, or variation—it makes everything else possible.

Now other Christians have claimed that, as a result of our rebellion and brokenness, we experience your love as wrath. This enigmatical perception arises from our disharmonic relations with you; it is where our feeling of your ostensible vengeance comes from. This may be true. But even here, the origin of the idea of wrath is on our side, not yours. With all that has been said about divine wrath, it seems that it is yet another apocryphal manifestation of unbelief. In this case the deleterious effect of unbelief becomes wickedly poignant as it begins to emerge within Christian consciousness—theological fear.

Christianity's obsession with your wrath has provided endless fields of fertile soil for the mustard seeds of fear. The Scriptures say that fear of you is the beginning of wisdom.[16] I disagree. The Scriptures should have said that fear of you is wisdom's end. I know that the idea of "fear" carries various meanings. I don't mean fear in the sense of our veneration of you or of the radicality of your otherness. I mean fear in the sense of being terrified of you, an emotional state of impending horror.

Fear of that foreboding nature threatens, not instructs.

---

16 Psalm 111:10.

It prohibits, rather than promotes, understanding. Fear facilitates coercion, not good judgment. Fear is conceived from imperfect love, and where love remains imperfect—that is, as in ourselves—fear abounds.[17]

Wisdom is conceived in your perfect love, not in fear, though Christianity has taken the errant biblical verse and made fear pivotal in the transformative phases of the soul. It's as if the internal disturbance of fear were like a musical arrangement—a music with abrupt starts and stops of cacophonous tones with no rhythm. Its chilling sounds and menacing pitches seize the soul with a foreboding harshness that radiates from a threatening God. The listeners fear a holy consuming fire awaits, not to devour but to deplete them until all that remains are seared selves, alone with suffering as their only companion. Yet, all the while the dark music of fear forges the infrastructure of the soul and lays the groundwork for a frightened response to the terror of the divine address. Then suddenly harmonious transitions of sweet, soft sounds are born, mellifluous melodies flow from a soul once paralyzed by divine dread. Once the acoustics of fear have been transfigured into serenity, your horrors can be averted by a timid answer of

---

[17] I am indebted to George MacDonald for this idea that he beautifully expounds in his sermon entitled "The Fear of God." MacDonald, *Unspoken Sermons: Series II,* 314.

faith. The soul has been delivered from an endless hell as the silken symphony ushers in the assurance of an endless heaven, but still there is an occasional echo of those dark sounds of fear to remind Christians of their destiny if the price for their wickedness and sinful condition had not been discharged through the work of Christ.

Fear of you is the elementary predicate for much of Christian theology. It is the seminal motivation for our inceptive return to the divine. Our embryonic reply to you is born out of trepidation because we see you as a threat, not to our freedom but to our very existence. Fundamentally, we are afraid of what you will do with us. I suppose our inchoate address to you from a mental state of anxiety is understandable. However, the anxiety never fully decomposes; its relics shape how we genuinely see you.

Perhaps that is why we are unable to believe in who you are and what you are like. Unbelief created and sustained by fear inhibits the truth that each and every person is conceived in your thought—the divine womb, as it were—with the eternal placentary nourishment of love and delight. There is no incorporeal evolution of our being within your heart; we are there, fully and completely and perfectly, not of necessity, an awful thought, but aesthetically—a creative act of sheer pleasure, not of duress. The beauty of this is accessible, even though it's an unspeakable reality.

Another source of our unbelief that distorts how we see you lies in our tendencies to mentally remove perceptions of unpleasant discrepancies among things we hold dear. Humanity's ability to resolve discrepancies between belief and fact through rationalization has been around for a long time. The earliest creatures sought no intellectual harmony when internal contradictions arose from their first metaphysical speculations. Such incongruities were not so much of any concern as they were inconspicuous. But at some point cognitive dissonance must have been elevated from mere inconsistencies between expectation and reality to the more vexing inconsistencies between spiritual beliefs and historical facts.

As a conjecture, when a child of our earliest predecessors died, grief stood alone as their only emotional reaction. But somewhere along the way, someone wanted to explain the discrepancy between expectancy and actuality. This desire for explanation must have been one of the initial strategies used by humanity to minimize the dissonant gap left by mere emotional sorrow. Of course there's nothing about the discordant feeling itself that necessarily ensures the truthfulness of the explanation. Moreover, the opportunities for extravagant rationalization grew as the discontinuities between belief and fact, each endowed with theological content, became more extraordinary.

At the time of the cross, the contradiction faced by the apostles was, to be sure, overwhelming. They had fled. But, in their case, the dissonance was created by their belief in a political savior, contrasted with their tormenting present reality of having followed a now dead one. That internal conflict must have been deepened by the sorrow of having lost a beloved teacher and friend. Things changed dramatically after the resurrection. Their savior was now alive. But the apostolic dissonance experienced at the cross had been overshadowed in later Christian traditions by a much deeper dissonance created by the need to explain why your son was crucified at all.

It's unclear when the doctrine of substitutionary atonement began to crystalize in early Christianity. According to the Scriptures, the basic idea of a sacrificial death for your benefit seems implicit in the story of Cain and Abel, as well as your directive for an offer of that nature.[18] Of course, no Old Testament story captures the imagination of Christians as a predicate for the crucifixion of your son more than the adventure of Abraham and Isaac. Ultimately, Moses standardized the slaughter of animals as

---

18 Genesis 4:3–7.

atonement for the sins of Israel as an annual event. After Christianity began, some of the early church fathers saw the crucifixion as your victorious defeat of Satan. Others combined the incarnation and crucifixion as a divine recapitulation of humanity. And yet others took quite literally some of the apostolic sayings as confirmation that your son's death contained not only a vicarious element but also a punitive one.

That said, with centuries of Jewish ceremonious tradition of sacrifice at the disposal of the apostles, believing that you had actually commanded its form, substance, and implementation, it was a natural step for them to cloak the cross with a sacrificial meaning. Although variations of this theme emerge in subsequent centuries, the fundamental interpretation has remained the same—Jesus Christ was crucified for the sins of the world.

It seems to me, my God, that this is when the fallacy was born. The apostles and early church had constructed a bridge between a mountain of belief and a mountain of fact over an abyss of contradiction and divergence. But "for they know not what they do."[19] The plans and specifications for the engineering were defective from their inception. The raw materials for the construction all shared two principal

---

19 Luke 23:24 (KJV).

ingredients—unbelief in the fundamental character of your love and the need to squeeze you into our rationalizations for suffering. The end product of early Christianity's labor was the crucifixion of your character. The desire for explanation overtook the need for Christ-like faith, with shredded pieces of your nature floating in its wake.

There is only one way to traverse the gulf of discrepancy between a belief in your son and the fact of his crucifixion while remaining true to your goodness. There's only one answer to a Christian's perception of disproportionality between your eternal son and your crucified son. It's a childlike belief that nothing is difficult for you, that nothing can obstruct a God who loves and gives out of his transcendence. All of creation reveals moment by moment that you are capable of doing something without cost. It's a simple recognition of who you are, uninterrupted by unnecessary intervals of theological explanation composed to remove the dissonancy, not of things inexplicable, but of things that require no explanation at all.

There may have been other factors and forces in play as the theology of the cross evolved. But it's my belief that unbelief in your true character, once the malignancy took root, spread unmercifully until its illusions of debt, wrath, punishment, and suffering, among others, eclipsed our original, simple faith, the kind of faith a child has when reaching out with guileless ease to take the hand of the father, as Christ himself unambiguously proclaimed to be the only way into your kingdom. I am making no appeal for an immature and visionless faith. But I repudiate the sophistry of unbelief spun by those Christian thinkers who, even more so than the Apostle Paul's reprobate, have "exchanged the truth of God for a lie."[20]

To believe that without the crucifixion there would have been no atonement, forgiveness, or victory over sin, to believe that all of our debts from sin were paid by Christ on the cross, to believe that because of your holiness you cannot behold us or be with us as your sinful creatures, to believe that you are wrathful, to believe that your justice requires the uttermost punishment, not of the sinner, but of your son, to believe that the cross was indispensable to our justification before you, to believe that you have not done and cannot do anything for nothing, or to believe any of these things on the authority of Scripture is to exchange the truth of who you are for untruth. It's itself a sin. It's a punishment of our own making. Those beliefs, which are really unbeliefs, are hostile to you; they misunderstand you. If any of these beliefs approached your

---

20 Romans 1:25.

truth, a message of septic news, not of good news, would be the refrain for our restless, rebellious souls.

In recent times, interpretive approaches to the crucifixion have become more integrated and balanced, symphonizing diverse biblical imagery.[21] From the cross, your son traversed the Red Sea of sin and death to deliver the captives, and left the Godless enemy drowning in his wake. He recapitulated the old Adamic nature of rebellion and disobedience into a new Adamic nature of submission and obedience. With the unforgettable marks of his ransom, he assaulted the gates of hell to rescue imprisoned souls. He shouldered and embraced the astronomic weight of divine judgment upon all sin and guilt, and enfolded it within your infinite mercy. The precious blood of his perfect sacrifice crushed all demonic forces, rectified all of creation, and proclaimed your kingdom where his cross will forever reveal your righteousness.

The underlying tendency in this layered approach of multiple images and metaphors is a shift away from the predominately penal aspect of the earlier reformed theology of the cross and a more focused shift toward the manner of your son's death—a Godless, shameful, degrading,

---

21 As a wonderful example, see the beautifully written and comprehensive book by Fleming Rutledge, *The Crucifixion: Understanding the Death of Jesus Christ* (Grand Rapids, MI: Eerdmans, 2015).

and dehumanizing crucifixion, a mode of execution commensurate with the depths of our fallen condition. Christ undertook the cross not only to consummate the ultimate exchange of the glory of his divinity for the curse of the law, but to deliver, rescue, and heal us from it. We are encouraged not so much to analyze the cross as we are to dwell in it and to allow it to dwell in us, to rejoice in its restoration more so than in its retribution.

Ironically, it is the crucifixion of Christ that makes Christianity, not a religion, but a unique irreligion. For no religion has its God crucified to save the world. The Hindu Vedas may have the god Purusha engage in the self-sacrifice of his anthropomorphic members in order to create, but only Christianity offers up Christ as a crucified criminal as the path to atonement and redemption.

But because I see divine injustice and unreasonableness in each of the three principal themes of atonement, then to search for a meaning of the crucifixion by integrating or blending elements of the themes into a rich, layered, and ambitious narrative leads me to the same dead end—a God who must appeal to savagery to achieve his desires. This combinatorial approach to the cross serves only to proliferate the fallacies within the atonement themes and to continue to degrade your character. To downplay the penal, punitive, and retributive features of substitutionary atonement is a modest improvement. But by the same token, it requires no intellectual ingenuity to recognize that to refocus one's attention on the Godless, shameful, and dehumanizing nature of the crucifixion is an emotional movement designed to induce divine meaning and significance where none otherwise exists. After all, a harmful character remains harmful even if it is clothed with a thematic and poetical narrative replete with passionate and metaphoric imagery.

Furthermore, when one inquires about how the shameful death of your crucified son or the utter dehumanization of Christ on the cross actually restores our relationship with you, the inquisitor is typically urged by pastors and theologians to take comfort in the customary platitudes—the mystery of God and the inadequacy of human language. They will insist, however, that there's one absolutely crucial point about your mysterious ways in the crucifixion that is crystal clear: The way of the cross with all of the unspeakable Godlessness which your son endured was, from top to bottom, all around, and through and through, a full Trinitarian act of God the Father and God the Son through the power of God the Holy Spirit.

So you have allowed your creatures an obscure glimpse into the unknown deep being of the Godhead so that we may cling with all of our hearts to the mysterious truth that the Trinitarian way of reconciling our fallen nature to your holy nature is by dehumanizing the second person of the Trinity through the most scandalous and disgraceful method available during the third decade of the common era. This is how we are recapitulated, rectified, restored, and redeemed by you, how we are healed, how you defeated the alien powers within our universe, how we are delivered from the curse of the law, and how your love for us, the worst of your creation, is revealed. You, as love itself, as goodness itself, together with the only begotten of that love and goodness, must become internally horrified by brutalizing your son on the cross to fulfill your love and goodness toward us. Before you can save us, you must scandalize yourself.

What can I say? It is agonizing to think about the madness of it all, the human intellectual equivalent of excrement in an attempt to understand you. I cannot inhabit this narrative, nor can it inhabit me. It is a narrative where the truth of your character and belief in that truth are sacrificed by Christianity because it believes, among other things, that the meaningless suffering of your son is itself insufferable. It is a narrative where Christianity thinks so little of you.

All of this means that the suffering and death of Christ on the cross accomplished nothing within the

Godhead. I say this without any apology for the trauma of my brethren. No debt was paid, no penalty endured, no sin forgiven, no punishment inflicted, no substitution made, no atonement effected, no wrath appeased, no justice satisfied, no victory obtained, no soteriology consummated, and nothing new established or inaugurated. Those lifeless spiritual transactions, vapid of any efficacy, barren of Trinitarian splendor, unendowed with the potency of your nature, empty of your goodness, and uninhabited by your love, justice, and mercy, not having been evacuated of such qualities by faithlessness, but having always been vacant in their originality, are the articulations of unbelief.

These articulations are the ultimate sign of dismayed souls who are impregnated with the psychological instability of oppressive theological dread and needless theological dissonance, who cannot live with any ambiguity or uncertainty in their relations with you, and who prefer the repetitive regurgitation of obsolete theological explanations to the simplicity of obedience. They will not allow you to replace the scriptural promise of heaven by oneness with your being. Their present spiritual reality consists of a circumscribed hope in a circumscribed God who will take them to a circumscribed place.

Dull souls, harnessed and immobilized by an inextirpable fallacy that is more pronounced than the elementary unsoundness of a fool who says in his heart there is no God,[22] insist that to be saved a person must accept their interpretive template of your redemptive activities on the cross. These dullards think that to accede to their strict explanation of your salvific plan is to place authentic and efficacious trust in the crucifixion, all premised on the belief that a suffering God is the key to a world in desperate need of redemption. For them, without suffering, without the blood of your son, there can be no forgiveness or salvation.

It is not a question of your knowledge, power, or benevolence for such Christians. They believe that you are all-knowing, all-powerful, and all-benevolent. So the approach you took on the cross to remove their sin from your mind, as you gaze upon them from heaven and indwell them on earth, does not reflect a deficit in your omniscience, omnipotence, or omnibenevolence. To the contrary, a battered, bloodied, and breathless Christ is an emphatic endorsement of those qualities. According to these Christians, the crucifixion is a revelation of the God you are in your sovereignty and glory, in your knowledge, power, and benevolence, without defect or deficiency, a

---

22 Psalm 14:1.

divine unfolding in time and on the cross of your character, nature, and being in eternity.

This incredible conviction raises a fundamental question: Is there a parent on the planet who has a fragment of reasonableness who would honestly prefer a God who must crucify his only son in order to forgive the guilty over a God who can and does forgive without a cost of violence, much less than at a cost to himself or his son? If a Christian parent knew that torturing one child to death would wipe away all the sin of the world and fully reconcile humanity to you in everlasting harmony, would they do it?[23] I doubt it. Every such parent would consider the demand unreasonable. "Only God can satisfy the unreasonable demand," they maintain. So, does their reasonableness exceed your reasonableness?

If Christians think that the parent-child analogy is too flawed or weak to accurately depict the relationship between you and your son, then they should consider the positively perfect analog of Trinitarian life in all of its diversity: creation. Think about the universe, the utter incomprehensibility of its magnitude, constitution, and forces, the strangeness of its energy and objects, the birth,

---

23 This is the question that Ivan asked Alyosha in Dostoyevsky's *The Brothers Karamazov*.

life, and death of its stars, its expansion, movement, emptiness, darkness, and age, the mathematical nature of its language. Consider something more familiar and accessible but equally magnificent: the earth. Flirt with the slow and precipitous changes in her structure, constituents, and history, the vast diversity of life that occupies her skies, surface, and depths, the stunning radiance of her divergent topography.

They should ask: Does the God who creates this unspeakable splendor with the spoken word require the unspeakable violence of the cross to redress human wrong? No! It's irreconcilable with your character. You love, and as every Christian should know, it is the very nature of divine love that "it keeps no record of wrongs."[24] No divine mechanism is required to effect the omission. No divine shame or scandal is a prerequisite to the exclusion. Your love just forgives and deletes.

If salvation from sin were accomplished by a violent assault upon your son, then your love and justice would not be confirmed but contradicted. This is why salvation thus explained is a dead end, not a mere impasse to a deeper, richer relationship with you, but an endless adjournment of life itself where only vermicular religious

---

24 1 Corinthians 13:5.

activity adorns the spiritually dead. We must not believe that you hold out the promise of salvation to those who trust in the illusive finished work of Christ on the cross. There's no such God.

The more appropriate and fulfilling word here is "redemption," not "salvation." The idea of salvation, at least in a fundamentally Protestant sense, has been so undressed of its grandeur, denuded of its restorative quality, and emptied of its divine intimacy that salvation has become merely a duplicitous rescue from hell, an idea well suited for those who see you exclusively as a God of deliverance, not from their poor selves, but from an undesirable domicile. And to compound this pauperized vision of you, they insist that a crucified Christ is the only exodus from the incendiary underworld.

Redemption—that is, salvation properly understood—has nothing to do with a change of eternal neighborhoods. It has everything to do with an unremitting contemplation, integration, and reiteration by us of your love, justice, and mercy, a ceaseless expanding unanimity of us with you and each other. Redemption deals with us seeing things as you see them, feeling things as you feel them, hearing things as you hear them, and touching things as you touch them; it is an undisturbed coalescence of our being with yours, a true reconciliation of us with you and each other—not one where you simply declare or pretend that it be so because of some historical event, even the crucified and risen Christ. Our redemption—its universal scope, its investiture, its assurance, and its endless completion—abides within your Trinitarian nature, not within a set of preordained earthly transactions. The cross removes no disruptions of sin that frustrate the fulfillment of that purpose. Obedience does. It can transform our world.

That may be the most uninspiring claim I make in this prayer, particularly given the fact that these days the idea of obedience has not only vanished from our conceptual understanding of freedom, but is seen as a repulsive restraint of our self-autonomy and self-actualization. A transformative obedience in our current cultural or theological climate may be considered as effectually offensive or ineffectually laborious, but I see it as inevitable because our desire and love for you cannot ultimately succumb to the negative forces of secularism or religion. We must understand and believe—that is, have faith in—who you truly are. Faith, hope, and love. The greatest of these is not love but faith. If we have faith in the truth of your character, the other two virtues will come.

CHAPTER 4

The Scripture

Dear God, there's no challenge to this prayer that can harness the energy, emotion, and extravagance of the Christian mind so well as the authority of Scripture. Advocates of substitutionary atonement who glimpse at a sentence or two of this prayer, or just the title alone, would rapidly summon the traditional apostolic curse under the rule of Scripture. I understand the intense loathing. If I had read this prayer a few years ago, I would have had the same expletory reaction.

Scripture reigns supreme in the Christian life.[1] It is

---

1 Unlike Protestantism, in the Catholic and Eastern Orthodox traditions, tradition itself (i.e., the life, practice, and teaching of the church) shares an equal footing with the authority of the Bible. Therefore, one may consider "tradition" included with each reference to "Scripture" or "Bible" in this chapter.

dynastic in power, influence, and durability. The incumbency of its proclaimed inspiration is inextricably embedded within the Christian soul. Man may have been the measure of all things to the ancient Greeks, but to Christians, Scripture is the measure of all things in man. It invalidates and surpasses anything considered unscriptural, whether physical or spiritual, natural or supernatural. The authenticity of any knowledge or understanding of you, man, or the relation between the two belongs solely within Scripture's jurisdiction. Therefore, any intellectual venture outside those jurisdictional boundaries is speculative refuse, fit only for a slow flame. Any thought, idea, perspective, belief, or experience without the agency of Scripture is illegitimate and worthless. To ignore Scripture is stupidity, to betray Scripture is criminal, to refuse Scripture is blasphemy, and to abandon Scripture is despair.

Not only is Scripture a cardinal need of the daily life of the Christian, it's also the spiritual valency that unites the hearts and minds of Christians together to form the life of the church. It carries the benefits and burdens of her organization, administration, teaching, and sacramental practice. Although not always so, particularly within incipient Christian communities, over the centuries Scripture has ascended to the preeminent position in every aspect of Christianity. The relevancy of Scripture as a primitive testimony of Christ slowly surrendered to an inflexible, exclusive frame of reference. The process of canonization eliminated the diversity of thought and written proclamation in early Christianity about what your son said and did, and solidified the four corners of the New Testament for future generations. In more recent times, however, Scripture itself has become an object of idolatry for many Christians. One could say that prior to the Reformation, the church stood between you and the Christian, and after the Reformation, the Bible has stood between you and the Christian.

"The Bible says . . . " and "What does the Bible say?" have been the fatigued declaration and wearful inquiry of the believer, as if nothing else at all matters, as if everything else is of no eternal significance, and as if the metaphysics of existence and the ultimacies of purpose and meaning are solely found within the sacred text. The divine resolution of every personal, sexual, spousal, child, governmental, economical, cultural, or moral issue can only be obtained by scriptural examination and deliberation. Our only hope of deliverance from the perils of relativism is the unappealable authority and inimitable objectivity of Scripture, as it dispassionately moves under the power of your Holy Spirit within the precipices of the depraved soul to purge all subjectivities of individuality and to restore the absolutism of divine knowledge.

All of this Christianity would have us grip with an unyielding faith. Unfortunately for Christians, their theories of the divine inspiration of Scripture, whether of the fallible or infallible form, suffer from the same unbelief that engulfs their theories of atonement. As their unbelief requires them to believe in the impossibility of salvation without the crucifixion, so their unbelief requires them to believe in the impossibility of salvation without your holy words as recorded by divinely anointed transcriptionists. The one unbelief has as its predicate you in death; the other has as its predicate humans in death—a slow darkening and eventual demise of intellect, sensibility, imagination, and vision as armies of fixed words "eat out their substance."[2]

The theological incongruities born of such a faith are unparalleled. As if it were not enough for Christianity to believe in the substitution of the living God for us in its theory of the cross, Christianity must also insist upon substituting a historical God for the living God in its ideology of the Bible. You are a living, transcendent, but perfectly present God who interminably loves all of your creation from the excess of your outpouring beauty, a solely aesthetic movement, with no external compulsion. You are

---

[2] The Declaration of Independence (US, 1776).

too abundant, too generous, and too extravagant for our parochial and paltry minds. Plagued by a fear of theological indeterminacy, saturated with a desire for theological exactness, and absorbed with theological borders, we remain content only to live, think, and breathe within the boundary laid by inspired words spoken and written within a preordained past. We are unwilling to venture anything with you and too afraid to move beyond the printed pages, believing that you have absolutely nothing to say outside of canonical books. It's as if the thoughts and reflections of any person that are spoken aloud or become letters on parchment can capture for all humanity the truth of the unique relationship between you and each man, woman, or child. This relationship is impenetrable by any other person—a connection between divine life and created life of a special rhythmic vivacity that only you and the particular being you hold within your heart may share.

In the meantime, I hear caustic voices of anti-pluralists rising up from the depths of unbelief that are more unwilling than unable to accept the fact of their uniqueness. They cling to the falsehood that sameness, rather than difference, is the aphoristic form of truth. To them, the content of divine revelations must have meaning synonymic to all. It must be written, and it must be confined; otherwise, to them their belief would take on the character of unbelief as they drift through a precarious ocean of obscurity like a piece of dead wood, horrified by the absence of any landmass to absorb the waves of speculation, and seeing no place to anchor their aimless souls, although just beneath the disturbance lies an infinite intimacy.

Christians intoxicated with their Bibles are like the Pythagoreans who believed that the entire cosmos arose from the first four positive integers—one for the point, two for the line, three for the plane, and four for the solid. For the Pythagorean Christians, four particular books of the Bible represent the pillars of earthly life, the loaves of a Christian's growth and sustenance. The Gospel of John is the "point" where the divinity of Christ is declared; the Epistle to the Romans is the "line" upon which all fundamental Christian doctrine is devised and systematized; the book of Psalms is the "plane" that emblematizes the emotional life of Christians as they engage God and the world—affective disturbances and exhilarations, sorrow and contentment, praise and conviction, despair and hope; and the book of Proverbs finishes up their mathematical perspective of our three-dimensional world—the "solidity" of practical life. I suppose if Christians are of the reformed persuasion, the Epistle to the Galatians would replace Proverbs as the fourth cornerstone, because

Galatians supplies what they think is the infrastructural dichotomy for every moment of the entire Christian life: that Christians live every such moment within the realm of grace or the realm of law.

Just an abbreviated digression on this dichotomy, if I may, Lord. To essentially discount or evade with a sweeping grace the untempered complexities of how to live as Christ lived within this world subsumed with goodness, but also stuffed with badness, injustice, ambition, sickness, disability, and suffering, or to avoid thinking of how to be at one with you and our neighbor when our interiors are subject to psychological delicateness, cognitive defects, or emotional disorders, many of which are completely outside our self-determination, is to transfigure your grace into a foul, colorless, and suffocating solution. All this dichotomy does, other than to preserve the remains of faith intact, is seduce Christians on the front end and leave them destitute on the back end. There they are expected to always loiter within the shadow of the cross and think that if they can just reflect more on grace and less on law, they can minimize the radial distance between their lived experience and the cross of Christ. They believe if they accomplish this, then a magical transformation will take place within their being where they can obtain the righteousness they credit to you, a doctrinal approach as vacuous as it is fictitious. Clearly the appeal to many Christians of the grace-law perspective lies solely with its intimate identification with the weakness of the human condition—its starts and stops, progressions and regressions—and the repetitive human experience of resolving one bad habit only to discover a new one beginning to emerge. But those enticed fail to realize that the toxic nature of the dichotomy only preserves things as they are while killing the life within them.

The psychology of the culprit here is unbelief. The dichotomous approach deserts the truth of your character, especially when it comes to your expectations for us. The dichotomist thinks that your law demands nothing less than complete perfection on our part during every nanosecond of our lives, and that the slightest failure or misstep renders us unfit for your presence and your kingdom. With the inelasticity of this vision, the dichotomist cannot see that if you can provisionally accommodate sin, then you can take provisional pleasure in our intermittent obedience, without having the weaponry of punishment in the back pocket of your divine garments, without regard to our innumerable past failures, and without concern over our innumerable future failures sure to come. You are not preoccupied with our evil. Regrettably, many Christians think that you are, and then proceed to engineer ways to anesthetize your stress and alleviate your perplexity, as well as their own.

More to the point: Many Christians believe that to sort of gently move within your grace, unattached to any notion of process or self-improvement and without any effort at obedience, is the key to a relaxed, happy life in Christ. They insist that one must make no attempt to assimilate good works, righteousness, or virtues, because to do so is to live under the law. It is to be terrorized by the holiness of a judgmental God. Christians should only listen to the gospel, receive the crucified Christ and his grace, and trust your promise that one is righteous because of what Christ did. They should not even consider whether they have faith. Instead, Christians should abstain from putting faith in their faith. Just dwell in promise and grace. Well, as with faith, grace without works is dead.[3] In fact, I think the truth goes further than this because even truth itself without works is dead.

To return to the matter of whether Scripture indeed represents your unique word to humanity, it is of no provocative force to me to read or hear Christians engage in unbroken dialectic about the proper method of biblical exegesis. To some, inerrancy of the Bible is the exclusive

---

3 James 2:26.

perspective, a precise dictation from you to man of every word of every sentence of every paragraph of every page and of every book in all of their perfect grammar, syntax, order, and meaning. To others, the allegorical method is the most effective because it penetrates the grammatical surface of the text to the spiritual ideas and themes underneath. Yet to others, the historical-critical approach is far superior because it frees Christian doctrine from the entrenchment of the traditional and cultural context and consequently allows its meanings to evolve with changes in tradition and culture.

It is no surprise that the inerrantists carry a much more ponderous burden than the other exegetical methods. The scriptural material is diverse and disparate in content and context, spans centuries of time, addresses countless needs of various kinds, describes divergent pictures of you, and is in itself replete with deep inconsistencies and contradictions leaving an abundance of information to explain away. The inerrantists violate their core commitment by effectively adding something to the text that does not exist within it, because even the authors of the original fragments of Scripture that survive did not anticipate the canon. It is actually quite entertaining to hear inerrantists square off with the multiplicity of textual difficulties and attempt to elucidate a coherent and compelling story of you and your creation from beginning to end. This is why I take such delight in Marcion's attempt at scriptural coherency by basically eliminating about eighty-five percent of the Scriptures.[4] Although his conclusions were wrong, his intuitions were saintly.

None of this is really serviceable to my belief that there's no such thing as your written word. I am unconcerned that interpretive ambiguities abound within the Bible, that serious questions arise as to its genuine authorship and dating, and that scribes committed many insignificant and significant errors when editing and copying the Scriptures. I acknowledge that passages were deleted or added, or that meanings were lost or misappropriated when transcriptions were made from the original languages into other languages. It doesn't matter that the task of preserving the oral stories of Jesus's ministry intact as they circulated from person to person and from town to town for decades until the four Gospels were written or of ensuring divine accuracy and continuity in the recorded

---

[4] Marcion of Sinope, a second-century theologian who was a fundamental dualist, believed that the God of the Old Testament was not the God of Jesus. Marcion made the first formal attempt to establish a canon of scripture, which consisted of the Gospel of Luke and select epistles of the Apostle Paul.

word for thousands of years among a flawed group of Jewish and Christian minds seems too large or even impossible for you.

The reason why I hold in contempt the belief that any word contained in the Bible or in any other book, including this one, whether spoken or written by Moses, the prophets, the apostles, Christ, or anyone else, presents an absolute authoritative and unchanging word directly from your mind is because the ultimate meaning, purpose, destiny, or life of any human being cannot depend on what someone else said. It cannot be eternally resolved by what another person uttered two thousand years ago or two minutes ago, even if the utterance has in some sense inspiration in you. A verse in Scripture may judge me, convict me, comfort me, inspire me, instruct me, or guide me. It may produce despair, repentance, and hope within me. But my life comes from, is sustained by, and is contingent upon you, and only you. Everything else, including the Bible, is expendable and unrequired. In no other person or place may my life be found except your thought, and your thought alone.

If you had otherwise decreed, if you had made my life or destiny contingent on my intellectual ability to comprehend a few key phrases or parables cobbled together by your son to express noncontingent truth or to understand an ancient epistle written by the least of the apostles under your direction, it would have been an act of creative cruelty. It would have been but to breathe your spirit into the nostrils of the inhuman, a creation not from love but from lovelessness. "Let us make man, or something like it, in our image. Let us put them on a planet and allow them to stumble and despair. Let us give them a limited amount of time to see if, by chance, they come across and understand the only secret to restored life that we will place in one book. If they cannot, we'll destroy them or, better yet, torment them forever." That's hatred.

With a vigorous regretability, especially when it comes to an unparochial and unoppressed understanding of your love as embodied in creation, Christianity has placed a written text above and beyond your living effluence imparted to the dust of the ground. It has enshrined the Scriptures at the cost of disembodying and defiling the divine image within man, an image fused with human nature to resonate divine, dynamic, creative, and infinite activity, not to resound memorized passages. What was intended to be an endless search of sacred life has indeed become an endless search of sacred words. What was meant to be a mere departure point to the distant shores of life-giving spirit has become a harbor for the port of death-giving letters.

I intend a more radical distinction than the usual difference between the law of Moses and the grace of Christ, because even the idea of grace dies when the letter says that my freedom from sin may only be obtained if I endorse the doctrine of atonement. Rather than cultivate a belief in God, a faith in Christ, a stroll with goodness himself that refuses to cover the same ground, that always waits for a new scene, and longs for another story, Christianity insists on the same landscape, the same view, and the same narrative. Human participation in divine adventures of love and joy has been commandeered by a yawning boredom that spawns when one has anchored oneself to a canonical set of books and epistles.

We should not allow the Scriptures to put us in a state of tonic immobility as though we were a school of decumbent sea creatures suspended in the deep. Rather, the Scriptures should challenge us, aggravate us, stir us to action—not just to love, to goodness, or to feed the poor, but to question, to reflect, to move beyond their limitations, deficiencies, and promises. We should feel and reason our way to the truth of your character. We should recognize, as Christ did, that the Scriptures neither give nor contain life.[5] Our life comes from you. It is

---

5 John 5:39.

you whom we should seek, know, and understand. Those who believe that nothing can be known or understood of you apart from Scripture are mistaken. Their belief has become too strong for truth. But how can this be? Because the sheer strength of their belief, not the belief itself, is divine.

The Bible tells amazing stories, whether true or fictional, and offers guidance and instruction on how to live, think, feel, and prioritize. It records the contrasting ways men and women saw you, understood you, worshipped you, engaged you, obeyed you, and disobeyed you. The Bible contains some intense, personal narratives worthy of study, reflection, and devotion. To me, the Bible is a salient source of provocative thinking about you.

But its fundamental deficiency is that it is not rich enough nor could it have ever been so. Scripture was never intended as the final word on any topic, including you, Christ, or salvation, nor was it intended to map out our relationships with you. You are not confined by language, nor are we. If we fail to recognize the inherent limitations of language and we believe that our experience of you must be limited by our interpretations of a fixed text, then our Bibles become our idols. To put it another way, to deny inerrancy is not an affront to Scripture. It is simply a reasonable caveat about Scripture's inability to describe everything without remainder.

The problem is much deeper than the limits of language. The Bible cannot tell our personal stories. No words, even the words of Jesus, no matter how eloquent, penetrating, or convicting, can live and tell our stories. Only we can do that. Only we can go into the unique place of your heart each of us came from.

Scripture does not speak to every person, much less every Christian. It has no truth value for much of humanity. This is not a sin or proof of a hopeless world. It's a reflection of the measureless diversity at the heart of the Trinity. Because you are as you are, because you love as you love, and because your character is as it is, our relationship with you, not with biblical texts, takes primacy. You and you alone are the core of our being, and we must strive to personally encounter you, live from you, and enjoy you. If some Christians think that the only way they can accomplish those objectives is to engage the Scripture, then so be it. But what are we to think of the rest of your created humanity? What are we to make of the fact that in terms of time, most of humanity has lived without the Bible or any other religious text? Because of who you are, oh God, those questions give me no momentary hesitation or concern. Any dispensational perspective that you decreed on which side of the Bible timeline humans would be born, which would ultimately determine their fate with you, if and how they would be redeemed, as bankrupt of anything God-like as that perspective may be, fundamentally contradicts who you are. The inevitability of every person is not a matter of timing or texts. It is a matter of the timeless and unwritten Trinity. Our redemption and inheritance can be found only within your heart and the heart of your creation.

Redemption is not so much the process of you getting into us as it is us getting into you. Redemption is not the acceptance of Christ as our personal savior so that he may deliver us from the repercussions of our sin or the agonizing grip of hell. Rather, our redemption is the plenteous participation of each being, in all of its differentiation, its uniqueness, its irreplaceability, and most of all, its indispensability to our fellow creatures, in the life, love, and glory eternally exchanged among the Father, the Son, and the Holy Spirit. Any Bible-based doctrine or teaching uncommitted or superfluous to that end is a dilution, if not an outright evasion, of uncovenanted truth, an explanation subtlety sustained by the very thing it abhors—unbelief.

Those who are fanatically obsessed with their ultimate destination have reduced Christianity to the most selfish vision of salvation, where knowing and loving you, the desire to be like you, with an ever-expanding authenticity, are all but lost within the noxious atmosphere of narcissism. So long as the question "Am I eternally set?" has been definitively answered with an irreversible "Yes," there really is nothing more to salvation, or to you for that matter, than to petition you when in need and to sharpen and rehearse the personal skills of a religious impersonator, all the while maintaining a clear theological distinction between salvation and sanctification.

Employing Jesus's shredding ad hominem assault of the Pharisees but with a modest redirection,[6] I say, therefore, woe unto you idolaters of the Bible, worshippers of the cross of Christ, members of a false profession, devourers of the children of the most high, sowers of rotten seed, juveniles of *reptilia*, and progenitors of desolation. You shut up the kingdom of God against humanity with your exhausting explanations of the heartless necessity for the sufferings of our Lord. You traverse continents and oceans to convert an "unbeliever," who has no guile, who would rather die than harm his neighbor, and who is content with just knowing that God is good, into a "believer" who is now enchained by the illusion of his own depravity, enslaved to the evil idea that his forgiveness from God

---

6 Matthew 23:13–39.

depends upon the acceptance of your unconscionable doctrines, and vassalized to finance your empires built with the bones of dead men whom you have made twice as much the sons of hell. You swear that the living, reigning Christ is nothing without the two pieces of wood on which he hung. You swear by his suffering and death or by the crown of thorns on his head, but you will make no oath to the one who has always indwelt the temple and sat on the throne. You have neglected the law, rendered no justice, shown no mercy. You have no faith. Instead, you have buried each of these divine ideas underneath your theological sorcery, as you yourselves swarm over trivial proof texts like two-winged insects. It is of no moment to you whether you swallow a herd of ruminant quadrupeds. You enter the fields of harvest as well-groomed marionettes, manipulated from within your unclean selves, not orchestrated from above. And you anchor yourselves as incandescent monuments, adorning them with synthetic semblances of life, while God, like the mother who looks down upon the face of her despondent children, picks them up and embraces them close and tight, is spreading her transcendent wings to enfold the clutch within the only place of unbroken life and peace—her heart.

Remember what Jesus had to say to these memorials of theological fatuity: "You will see me no more."[7]

A ruthless search and scrutiny of only the leather-bound volume with gold-gilded pages constricts the optics of the soul where all that remains is a cataractal vision of God, a God who must function consistently with a closed set of myopic promises and expectations, a God who must proceed with his achromatic judgments against a cadaverous humanity in accordance with the Scriptures, a God who must correspond and harmonize with the biblical chronicle of his immanence and economy—who he is in himself and who he is with us, or a God who has entombed himself within the ossuary of Scriptures.

Steadfast deep dives into biblical texts—believing not only that they contain the very word of God because God has nothing else to say to his creatures, believing not only that they contain the bread of life, but also believing that without them there can be no life—asphyxiate the divine breath of our spirits which, according to Johannine mysticism, are to blow wherever they please, unforeseeably and unpredictably, with only their sound being heard.[8] The reality of the Christian spirit is much different, however.

---

[7] Matthew 23:39.

[8] John 3:5–8.

With its immense intellectual and emotional investment in the Bible, its cemented perspective on the source and exclusivity of Scripture, the spirit of Christianity has imprisoned itself within the intransigency of its own theological paradigm.

Father, I feel it's not so much that Christians do not want to breathe the infinite air of latitude and range when thinking of you as it is their fear of your fallout if they did. "With God all things are possible"[9] except one. It is impossible for you to create life out of love, to write a book, and then to make that life contingent on what the book says. That would be neither life nor love, but cruelty. And you are not cruel.

As I see it, Father, Christianity, especially the Protestant derivatives, should detoxify its addiction to Scripture, its consumptive enslavement to inspired words. Perhaps the most effective, if not only, way to achieve deliverance from Christianity's abusive idolization of texts is to come face-to-face with the truth: The Bible is not indispensable to you, to us, or to the divine life we share. Simply put, the Scriptures are disposable. They should be; they must be.

---

9 Matthew 19:26.

CHAPTER 5

The Meaning

When Christians hear that no spiritual transaction of any kind occurred on the cross, whether within the Trinity or between the Trinity and us, the questions they ask are: "Then why did Jesus die?" "If Christ bore none of my sin or its penalty, or that no forgiveness, substitution, or justification was conferred by his death, then what's the meaning of the crucifixion?" "What purpose did it have?"

The answer: none. Why do we need one? Contrary to almost two thousand years of church teaching and the fictive-inspired word of God beginning with Genesis straight through to Revelation, including the word of the apostles and even Christ himself, there is no inimitable meaning, purpose, or other momentous explanation for the cross of Christ. No mysterious, mystical, magical, or gnostic reason is hidden underneath the suffering of your son. You neither revealed nor consummated an epochal, crucial, or decisive breakthrough during the dark days of the passion.

The idea of meaning is secondary to the idea of "essence," as meaning is a frame of understanding that we impute to the inherent nature of a thing. So if a philosophical Christian were to ask, "What was the essence of the cross?" I would have the same answer: none. Perhaps the pieces of wood have essence, or the nails have essence, or the blood has essence, but the crucifixion event itself has none. The execution of Christ on the cross is as insignificant as the execution of thousands of others during the Roman era. God the Father, God the Son, and God the Holy Spirit always already are God, and no essence of any earthly thing and no meaning of any historical event adds to or subtracts from that eternal truth.

Father, you did not change because of the cross. If the death of Christ on the cross had never transpired, or if Christ had died in some other way at the hands of the Jewish priesthood or the Romans, or if Christ had an Enochic[1] end—that is, had never died—you would have issued no new decrees for the destiny of humanity. Heaven would not be empty and hell would not be full. History would definitely have changed, but you would not. You would have remained the same, even as the Bible affirms.[2] And the same is true of your son. He has always been God.[3] He did not become the Christ, our messiah, because of his unique passage through time as a man. His death and resurrection were not qualifications that, by some mysterious divine alchemy, made him eligible to be our savior. Your son has always been our Lord and savior. Naturally and quietly, the lowest and highest of his human experiences, his humiliation in a disgraceful death and his exultation in a risen life, reveal a divine love that walks, a life to be enjoyed, not to be explained.

If a Christian advocates that the cross has always been a part of the divine scheme from the eternal beginning and therefore there was no further development within you necessary to save us, then your character would have always been treacherous. Duplicity is duplicity whether in eternity or in time. My oblation to you, my praise of you,

---

[1] A reference to Enoch, a person in the book of Genesis who apparently did not die but was taken up to the heavens.

[2] Hebrews 1:10–12.

[3] Hebrews 13:8.

is that you are good, that you are above change, and that your goodness is without mutation or refinement, utterly unpierceable by anything outside of you—humanity, the human condition, or sin itself.

All of this is to say that the cross was meaningless from your perspective. It was not necessary for you to be as you are. The death of your son did not intensify your love for us. It did not make you feel, think, or see differently than you have always felt or thought about us or seen us. It had no effect on your capacity, quality, or character in any way whatsoever. For me, this is why the meaninglessness of the cross is so essential. This is why your infinite power and the invincibility of hope for humanity lie at the foot of a meaningless crucifixion. The pointless cross discloses your glory. One could say that the meaning of the cross is its meaninglessness or that the purpose of the cross is its purposelessness.

Perhaps this will make Christians feel better about a vacuous crucifixion. When your perfect love meets the perfect hate of man on the cross, your love passes by the hate as if it were nothing at all. The ultimate manifestation of man's hate, the most severe display of human malignity, the sovereign expression of its wicked power and control, is to take a person's life. Whether it's jealousy, irritation, encroachment, hate, or some other evil motive, if one wants to get another person out of the way, then elimination by execution is the most effective. "Don't you realize I have power either to free you or to crucify you?"[4] But the infinite boundary of your love for your creatures empties this outermost boundary of man's iniquitous domain of its power. All that remains is God's grace.

Moreover, the early church fathers saw the incarnation of Christ as kenosis, an "emptying out" of his divine attributes, so that he may experience the human attributes of suffering and death. But even here, the more essential meaning of kenosis was an emptying out of any meaning of suffering and death, including his own. Your glory as seen in the cross is that your love is too strong for death.

There should be no implication here that your love had to engage the enmity of man in an all-out war with your son as the only carnage, no inference that man's rebellion perfected your love. You battle with no one—no principalities, power, sin, death, or even the free will of man. You are infinite, the only infinite. Everything else and everyone else are utterly finite and absolutely contingent. Their existence depends entirely on you as the potentiality and actuality of all else. Thus, any assault on you is the highest ineffectuality, an empty endeavor. Your

---

4 John 19:10.

response to the created is endless love, a love that is subject to no abatement by us or anything we can do or have done—even inflicting pain and death on your only son.

I do believe that the crucifixion is a historical fact. But I do not believe that the historical vicissitudes of our Lord's means and mendicancy, merriment and misery, including his misery on the cross, corresponded with any measurements of your love or any methodical or desultory vacillations between your love and wrath for your creatures. The life of your son, dear God, was entirely filled with you, even while he hung on the cross. Your son's death was not a reflection of any Trinitarian change to accommodate a sinful people that you happened to love. The crucifixion was not evidence of some grand scheme to atone for the evil constitution and ways of man. It was a fact, an event in history, but it did not embody a divine correction.

The cross of Christ was nothing new for you. You did not, through your son, enter into an untouched experience, a neoteric advance into the unknown, or a pristine pastoral encounter with suffering in order to unlock your pardon. There is no depth with you, oh God. Your infinite being is an endless surface of unbounded love where the geodesic lines of peace and purpose for all of humanity are unalterable, and the nicks and notches of our intricate iniquity or the hollow depressions of our selfishness do not stop them. This is where the supremacy of the cross resides, on the surface, not hidden so that the church may extract hideous explanations. It is a surface that reveals a continuing revelation of who you are, what you're like, and what you have always done before your spirit moved across the deep, exchanging perfect love within the Trinity that everlastingly erupts in a profusion of love for us to receive and engage as we are drawn into divine life. This is so much more than the mere absence of tears, pain, and death. This is life so rich, abundant, diverse, and selfless that there's no place for tears, pain, or death. There's no time for insecurity, anxiety, fear, or the other pestilences of imperfect loves. The perfect love of God expels all venom and violence.

To refuse to see that the meaning of the cross is its meaninglessness is to dishonor you. It is to oppose your love, refute your goodness, and disparage your character. It is to hold your sovereignty in contempt. It is to take refuge with the inventions of Christianity. It may signal an impregnable faith in the sanctity of Scripture and doctrine, but to treat those referents as trust in the one and only living God is a derailment, a full stop made to look like a movement of a life of faith with a fluency in scriptural language and with the fictitious garments of vicarious atonement and imputed righteousness.

I suppose a Christian might say that I am a radical eliminative spiritualist—like an eliminative materialist who desires to eliminate certain common words, such as "hope," or theological words, such as "propitiation," because they are reducible to the neurological interplay of biochemical events. This may be an accurate characterization. For me, all meaning, to be meaning at all, must be found within and derived from the eternal life and love of the Godhead, not from grand themes infused into historical events by those who cannot countenance historical remainders, the arbitrary unfolding of genuine creaturely freedom, or from a God who supposedly creates and directs every single natural event for his purpose, including the flight paths of sparrows. If this is how your sovereignty works, then creation would have no real meaning. The heartbeat of humanity, its freedom, its aesthetic, would only be the needless repetition of insolvent ideas, the barren discharges of a tautologist God.

It's impossible for you to create anything that does not reflect your image in some way. You are the ground of our being. We exist because we participate in your being. The human being, more than any other creature, possesses an image closer to the image of you, and requires an enormous amount of room to realize his or her freedom and meaning from you.

I have no doubt, Father, that the meaning for a human is particular to that person alone, for he or she stands singularly in the universe of your heart as the only one who can understand it. Do we not spend much of our time in search of universal meanings of episodic installments of history instead of excavating our own souls to find the diacritic meanings that you have endowed to us and sharing them with others? Well, whatever those meanings turn out to be, I am confident of one thing: None of them will reveal suffering as its monolithic intention, but all of them will reveal that your character and love are absolute and unmovable, free of all contingency.

If there were eternal significance to the suffering of Christ—divine acclimatizations within you—then there's no valid reason to think the Holocaust or any other atrocity of mankind contained no abiding gravity. In other words, if your son was fully human as we are, then there's no reason the suffering of innocent men, women, and children at the hands of their fellow demented creatures would carry any less significance than the suffering of your son. Sinless perfection adds absolutely nothing to tip the scales in favor of Christ. It may make the pain more exquisite and outrageous, but it does not change his essence.

As for those human horrors, the outcry for an explanation or anointed benefit of such senselessness reaches a crushing decibel. An explanation offered from a Christian perspective based on a delicately woven intense love of God who orchestrates those atrocities to accomplish the divine omega is to hear galactic garbage. It is to hear not love but intrinsic evil. The intellectual imperative to take God's love into the core of those wicked acts and create a purpose for every suffering endured by every person, and thereby form an intricate crochet of God's majestic pattern, qualifies as a legitimate obsessive-compulsive disorder, which is in desperate need of medication or a measure of pliant thinking. Heavenly Father, I do not believe that this kind of explanation represents a choice for us between a changing God infatuated with control or a moronic God submerged in contingency. It is fundamentally a choice between a robotic creation or a free one. Human freedom guarantees deviancy. As with the Holocaust, the crucifixion was a random event of pure evil, an arbitrary human act of monumental proportions, to be sure, but neither incident was suffused with a divine imperative or meaning; they were only dimorphisms of the same species of rotten human nature.

After the Holocaust, a Jewish philosopher wrote: "Dietrich Bonhoeffer has written that our problem is how to speak of God in an age of no religion. I believe that our problem is how to speak of religion in an age of no God."[5] The philosopher was both lamenting and rejoicing about the void in the human experience of the divine presence that was left by the death of a God who acted as the world's ultimate architect. Now the problem seems to be how to speak of God in an age of too much religion. We have an overabundance of theological doctrine and explanation. Much of it begins with an ugly and unpleasant God. This is particularly the case after a tragedy occurs. As we wail, cry, and scream, looking for answers, the doctors of divine doctrine inundate us with their cruel assurances that you are the ultimate purpose for the calamity. They think that without a divine purpose underlying every event within the drama of human history, your sovereignty, power, and goodness are compromised. They fail to see that what makes your sovereignty, power, and goodness a reality to us is the aesthetics of our created freedom, not in the diminutive sense of unrestraint or lack of coercion, but in the artistic sense of our eternal realization and disclosure of your idea of us, an idea that did not arise on a slow afternoon of Trinitarian discourse but one that has always been in your mind. If Christians want a fine-tuned universe,

---

5   Richard L. Rubenstein, *After Auschwitz* (Indianapolis: The Bobbs-Merrill Company, Inc., 1966).

they should study physics, not theology. You orchestrated neither the Holocaust nor the crucifixion.

Now the Apostle Paul, an original, radical, and creative thinker and the first of all great theologians, characterized the cross as a stumbling block to the religiously prideful and the intellectually sophisticated, presumably because the violent narrative of your son's crucifixion opposes those preoccupied with their own self-righteousness or wisdom.[6] Maybe not enough can be said against human arrogance. But here again, a violent cross is not the solution to the swagger of humanity. It opposes not only self-importance, but also selflessness, love, and goodness. A violent cross defies even you.

Paul's characterization was a temporary departure from the core of his message. He, along with other writers of the New Testament, urged the worshippers of the risen Christ to trust Christ with their lives, not to live in his passion, and not to dwell in the shadow of his cross, nor to sequester their hearts and minds within a single interpretation of one historical event, but to engage the living Lord in the immediacies of daily life. Like meaning, a real, honest-to-God trust has nothing to do with a conviction that any of the archival facts concerning our

---

6   1 Corinthians 1:18–25.

Lord's passion did something to you or revealed something that you did for us. Rather, trust is a way of life with no expectation on your part that we must preoccupy ourselves at every moment and every turn with an awareness that we are depending upon you. We are under no obligation from you to direct all of our efforts to maintain an uninterrupted stream of conscious reliance upon you. Our mental life was not made to remain in a state of divine fixation. Attention, forgetfulness, concentration, interruption, continuity, and discontinuity—in short, change—comprise the natural constitution of our minds.

I have found that the most profitable moments of trusting you come when, in monopolizing routine or in the chaos of personal difficulties, everything seems to slow to a glacial pace. It's almost a peaceful discontinuation of all surroundings except a few of the poetical movements of nature, such as the stillness of unrippled waters not yielding to a light breeze breathing across the tops of high trees. A wide, warm quietude ushers in a feeling of a loss for thoughts, not so much a loss for words, and then suddenly the divine voice brings the eternal message robed with the sensation that: Everything will be okay. It will be okay. To know this with all of one's being is to trust you. This radical trust transforms the way we see you, oh God, the way we approach you.

In the meantime, our endless search for indurate, invulnerable, and infinite meaning should be along the path of understanding your Trinitarian life, that intimate and bountiful communion, ecstasy, and joyfulness shared with each other, where the superabundance of aesthetics pours out in a creative act of love so that the fullness of your life may be shared with us, not from need but from pleasure, a sheer delight of allowing us to participate in the freedom and fellowship of the Godhead. That's grace. An undeserved divine benefit procured by the expenditure of the rich life of your son is the antithesis of grace. It's disgraceful. But the beautiful light of Trinitarian life extinguishes the darkness of a scandalous cross. We, who are made in your image, can fully and wholly assume that grace.

We are not the residuals of your love, nimieties of a divine afterthought, leftovers of an exhausted God, but the deliberate act of generosity, a predestined intention of pure gift, an indestructible bestowment of love, purpose, and meaning for us to see, feel, and live. The God you are should be pursued relentlessly, not the God assembled by the unbelief of man. That God is hidden behind a curtain of darkened explanation drawn by the faithless squanderers who are far worse than the prodigal son. They squander your green pastures and still waters, your very love, beauty, and peace, in the valley of the shadow of death—the uncultivable, hardened, and harsh countryside of their doctrinal crag.

We should rejoice in the truth that you had nothing to work out on the cross. We should be glad that nothing required you to scale a mythical wall of wrath to drench your sinful creatures with mercy. We should be overcome with joy that no doorway into your heart is framed in suffering, and we should glorify you because of your character, not because we have been able to transfigure, by theological ingenuity, the worst that man had to offer two thousand years ago into divine expediency. So, the meaning of the cross is nothing at all because of everything you are.

CHAPTER 6

The Testimony

It would require formidable effort for me to fabricate a personal story of my Christian experience that surpasses the level of dreadful dullness of what has actually transpired in my spiritual journey. But thankfully, being dismissive is of divine incipiency. I feel relieved that many of the twists and turns of my Christian history, as well as those inertial periods when experience seemed to retain a state of rest, may be dismissed as inconsequential. Generally, however, my spiritual past seems to have reflected a transformation of thought, faith, and experience similar to several of the significant movements in history—patristic, reformation, dark ages, renaissance, enlightenment, romantic, and postmodern, but certainly not with the same depth, scope, and intensity of those movements.

I was born, christened, and raised in the Greek Orthodox Church during my patristic period. At my age, with my gossamery mind, I recall very little of this part of my religious upbringing. As a Sunday school student, I mastered the art of coloring between the lines of the obligatory pictures of Old Testament stories—Adam and Eve within the Garden of Eden (post-fall, of course, lest the tender child should become too soon obsessed with certain anatomical features); Noah and the ark; Moses crossing the Red Sea; and David and Goliath. My general biblical knowledge was essentially limited to learning which books belong within the Old Testament and which belong within the New. I memorized the creeds. My lessons about Christ were traditional and rudimentary in form—he was your son, born of a virgin, crucified for our sins, and raised from the dead. Among all that, he performed some miracles and said some fairly enigmatic things. The liturgy, whose radial point has always been the transubstantiation of the elements, was spoken in Greek, a language I had not learned other than a handful of exquisite profanatory phrases. I suppose my biggest regret when I look back at this period of my Christian heritage is my failure to learn the Greek language and to understand what the great patristic thinkers and writers of the third, fourth, and fifth centuries had said about your nature and the nature of your son. I suspect, however, their opulent ideas would not have made a cosmetic furrow in my adolescent mind.

My reformation period began in my early teens. One Saturday afternoon, while walking through the woods, I invited you into my heart and presumably was born again, born from above by your spirit. This was an indispensable transactional moment without which, according to evangelical Protestants, a venue reversal from hell to heaven is absolutely impossible. The state of forgiveness from sin by the blood of Christ, the state of possessing your eternal life through the presence of the Holy Spirit, the state of justification and righteousness before your holiness, and the state of an itinerary change from endless torture behind your back to endless rapture at your feet all come down to a slice of Planck time[1] of a person's entire earthly existence, when they decide whether they say "yes" or "no" to the gospel. The ultimate finality and quality of all being, existence, and life ride on a person's single decision for those of an Armenian persuasion. For those of an Augustinian persuasion, as fine-tuned by Calvinism, that momentous decision is made by you, not by us.

---

1   An incredibly small unit of time defined by Max Planck, a German physicist, where just one second is like an eternity compared to that smallest unit.

Well, following my rebirth, I became addicted to the fundamentals and practice of evangelical Protestantism for a couple of decades. The addiction was harsh and its effects were gladiatorial. I became compulsively immersed in every form of Christian activity, and armed with the inerrancy of Scripture, I developed a militant enthusiasm to engage and convert the lost in schools, prisons, and shopping malls, always on a mission with the message. Little did I realize that my proselytistic crusades were merely expeditions to annoy and torment your creatures, not with the good news, but with disgusting news, a miserable message about a miserable God who cannot forgive and abide with the created without the blood of the spotless. But then again, if the destiny of every soul pivots around a simple and single decision made within this lifetime, and with no chance or opportunity for reconsideration thereafter, then being a witness for that truth made sense.

Besides my life of loudly declaring what I erroneously believed was truth, most of my time during the reformation period was consumed with prayer and Bible study, but more Bible than prayer. Personal contemplation of Scripture was my obsession. The sun rarely set on a day when I had not read and memorized some verses. I pored over the book from cover to cover countless times, with highlights, underlines, microscopic marginal notes, crisscross lines, and tarnished page corners. To enrich my understanding, I consulted popular commentaries, Greek and Hebrew lexicons, and other translations and supplemental materials. I had developed the ability to write on any Christian topic and cite one verse, if not multiple verses, from both Testaments after each sentence. Understanding the Bible had become my exclusive enterprise, so much so that I withdrew intellectually from every other field of study—history, literature, science, and mathematics. I suffered from that exodus. To this day, I still feel the need to make up the ground forfeited to years of intellectual mendicity within the presence, or should I say custody, of Scripture. Nevertheless, my reformation experience laid the foundation for how I saw you, why I believed you, and what I believed about you for the next twenty-five years.

Marriage, children, and exhaustion put an end to my personal reformation and ushered in the dark ages, or as the historians prefer to say, the early middle ages. As you know, this characterization is no bitter reflection on your institution of marriage or its seed. My spiritual pause arose from a new set of obligations, from a natural abeyance because of the gravitational force of selfishness, and from a spiritual subsidence. It was only logical for my traditional faith to erode when the divergence between the fundamentalist's perception of you and the wisdom of truth, its lack of excessiveness, its reasonableness, first appeared to me and began to grow. During this period of my life I retreated from all exterior parts of Christianity—church, worship, witness, prayer, and Scripture. My Bibles began doing what I suspect the Bibles of many Christians who are trying to save the appearance of spirituality do: collect dust as bookends on scarcely visited shelves but are typically enhanced with a piece or two of porcelain figures. My thoughts of you slowly began to vaporize, my convictions dissipated. Spiritual dehydration was the defining characteristic of this phase of my life. I had no thirst for the God I knew and no desire to revive any form of Christian practice. Occasionally I would attend a Sunday school class just to see what people were thinking, but I heard nothing new, only a tired repetition of the same old ideas with different words. The focal points of my life had become vocation and family, in that order. This state of affairs lasted for several years, but eventually my curiosity, the natural stirring of innate inquisitiveness within every soul, the heartbeat of knowledge, could no longer be ignored.

    I had begun to transition to the renaissance period of my life. I turned to philosophy. After a brief stretch of trying to understand how one could construct a philosophy of life out of earth, air, water, and fire, I decided to see what

Socrates, Plato, and Aristotle had to say. It was a lot. Richness, range, diversity, and practicality filled the pages, and pleasure filled my soul. It was a virginal delight to read the ancient philosophers who were obviously untouched by Christianity, but thankfully, they had touched the essence of Christianity. These philosophers were quite enjoyable to read despite the cacophonous rants of the purest of Protestants against the idea that some of the early Christian writers had absorbed too much Hellenistic culture or had consumed too much Platonism, always with the Pauline verse from the Epistle to the Colossians at their side—"See to it that no one takes you captive through hollow and deceptive philosophy, which depends on human tradition and the elemental spiritual forces of this world rather than on Christ."[2] Such Protestants always hold a deep disdain for the slightest deviation from Scripture. Of course not all philosophy is good; some of it is paltry; and some of it is downright brutal to digest.

After feeling my mind expand with the early philosophers, it was natural for me to move into my personal period of enlightenment, a time of reason as opposed to faith. I know that reason emerged in my life during this period similar to the way it did in European culture

---

2 Colossians 2:8.

during the seventeenth and eighteenth centuries. It had always been there—napping, arising, growing, and changing. But whatever the reason—perhaps my stubborn indifference to anything that had no clear foundation in Scripture finally surrendered, or maybe I had developed some neurotic self-hatred for allowing Christian tradition to demand so much of my potential experience that self-hatred became a catalyst for seeking out knowledge outside of biblical theology—I discovered the magnetism of science.

Science's ability to describe, explain, and predict with repetitive verification by experimentation is intellectually alluring and gratifying. And the attraction to that ability is caused by our elementary desire to better understand the world. The idea that science or the great scientific thinkers secretly planned to eradicate faith is false. Newton's theory of force and motion, Darwin's theory of natural selection, Einstein's theories of special and general relativity, or Feynman's theory of quantum electrodynamics did not encroach on the hallowed relations between God and man. Those scientists wanted to understand how the world works through the methods of science.

I don't mind admitting the temptation to believe that truth abides in science and nowhere else. While science illuminates with its coherent regiments, theology obscures with its caliginous rituals. It's easy to observe the power of scientific explanation. But it's difficult, if even possible, to recognize the power of theological explanation. To the extent I had perceived some insight about you, many times I could not help but think that it was all located within my imagination. I was curious if my spiritual speculations were only echoes of hope that ultimately truth dwelled outside the detection of my senses. I wondered whether my thoughts about you were just fabrications that not only was there something beyond the material world, but that the something saw and cared for me. That said, the question of your existence has never interested me. It is a relatively stimulating exercise to examine the various arguments for and against your existence, whether ontological, cosmological, teleological, or any of their logical derivatives. The question that became of intense interest to me, almost to the point of a tireless obsession, concerned what kind of God you were.

At the outset of my romantic period, I did not reappraise my system of values, nor did I fall in love with poetry and art. My emotions did not replace my rationality; I did not look at nature differently than I had before or wish to spend the rest of my days under an oak tree contemplating the simplicity of life. In fact, the only thing that excited me in my early forties was the same thing that made me salivate in my early teens—the female form. Only one constitutional shift had occurred within my being.

A massive displacement within my perception of you had materialized less than a year after my brush with romanticism. Only one man is responsible for this theological revolution—the nineteenth-century novelist and poet George MacDonald, a romantic theologian in every aspect of his thought and vision. To say, as MacDonald did, that when a girl dies she is not transported into the presence of God, but rather God is transported into the presence of the girl, takes her hand, and brings her home, is to express a divine movement of heroic romance. It is not a spontaneous or unfamiliar act, but one eternally rehearsed within the natural adoration of the Trinity where each cherishes, and is cherished by, the other, without end. I know this will sound anthropomorphic, but I believe that you cannot stand for us to be in disharmony with you and that you long to be pleased with us. You want us to know and feel that we are pleasing to you, and you want us to share in the delight you have with one another in the Trinity. You will not rest until those divine aesthetics have been achieved once and for all, everywhere and with everyone.

C. S. Lewis may have been baptized by MacDonald's work into the fires of fantasy, but MacDonald baptized me into the blue flames of a romantic goodness, a goodness that always lovingly speaks down to us, a goodness that cannot do anything other than what is fair, decent, and rational. This goodness is incapable of violence or pretense when it comes to sin, because this goodness cannot save without the will and work of the sinner, a goodness that never gives up or gives in, and a goodness that is unbounded by time. If a person cannot see your goodness, if they insist on endorsing two thousand years of theological manipulations to make your biblically ascribed unconscionable acts conscionable, then they cannot see you. Honestly, they see the prince of darkness, of unreasonableness, and of insensibility. This monarch is not some demonic spirit who is assailing their faith at every turn of weakness or some sovereign confirmation of the strength of their faith amid the satanic assailant; rather, it's the decrepitude of their own unbelief.

MacDonald was not a systematician or a professional theologian, or a friend of biblical doctrine. But the breadth and depth of his view of you was not only pervasive and piercing, it was original, alive, and full of practicality. He believed that to live truly was more important than to think correctly. The importance of obeying you over explaining you runs through his work like a roaring river. I now understand why C. S. Lewis said that MacDonald was closer to your spirit than any other Christian writer he had ever read. It has been said that some books should be tasted, some should be swallowed, but others must be chewed and digested.[3] There's no doubt in my mind in which category MacDonald's *Unspoken Sermons* falls. I had a feeling of regret each time I read his book because I knew I would never find and read anything like it again. I didn't want the end of the book to come.

During my period of romanticism, one puzzling obstacle kept surfacing, which ultimately moved me into my period of postmodernism. Here again, MacDonald was the stimulant. When I pondered the vastness of humanity, with its innumerable faces, abundance of souls, all with so many ideas, opinions, meanings, and feelings, I could not find a satisfactory common denominator of truth. There was no universal meaning that could possibly tie all of those countless differences together into one grand metanarrative. There was no approach of thought that could begin to eliminate the fragmentary nature of humanity.

The question that occurred to me was: Why should we remove fragmentation? What's wrong with it? Why must universalism eclipse particularity? I think the answer to these questions is that the universal and the particular, sameness and difference, belong to the Trinity, but

---

3 Francis Bacon, a sixteenth-century English philosopher.

without competition or enmity. You, with the Son and Holy Spirit, share your life with the other in an absolute oneness and liberty with no need of synthesis or supplementation. It is a unity that just is. Here, like nowhere else, thought and language disappoint.

For those who implore metanarratives, here's one for reflection. Every person is an incomparable aesthetic presentation of an idea of love that God has, having no like or equal, utterly unparalleled. When the time comes, and it will, each person will be stripped spiritually naked, so to speak, and will stand alone, divested, and exposed before the creator with nothing—no parent, sibling, spouse, child, or friend; no religious text, creed, or doctrine; no assurance, promise, or doubt; no sin or darkness; no explanation, answers, or narrative; and no warmth from a memory or place to retreat. At that moment, each person will see you as you are and as no one else can, and will see themselves as they are and as no one else, other than you, can. This is the judgment of God, an encounter of pure beauty and peace with the creator. This is the perfect gift, not in the contemporary philosophical sense where gift is so divested of the ideas of recognition and reciprocity that it becomes a total unconscious event, but in the sense that the gift is full of desire and delight.

This metanarrative of gift must unfold with its eternal

compositions and infinite expressions, for it's an insuppressible moment where each person will learn to see his or her desire, need, and fulfillment as having a divine origin. At that time, each person will see themselves and their many characteristics as the heartbeat of God's thoughts about him or her, and they will learn not only to feel oneself into another but to love oneself into another, a tireless exchange of giving and receiving, of address and response. I do not know what the Apostle James meant when he wrote that "Every good and perfect gift is from above."[4] But as I see these visionary words, the gifts showered upon us from on high are our needs and neighbors, without which and whom our beings would have no meaning at all. This is the kingdom of God, a place where no one may "pass by on the other side."[5]

Father, I wish to say this to Christians. The bond between each of you, as well as every other human being, and God—whether you affirm it or deny it, whether you're unaroused by it or unaware of it—is indestructible. It comes into existence by the very eternal thought of God. God is saying, "I formed you within my heart, and my love has brought you forth. There's no power or

---

[4] James 1:17.

[5] A reference to the parable of the Good Samaritan. Luke 10: 25–37.

person, not even me, who can put an end to my bond with you."

This bond is as impenetrable by the outside world as a Christian is. Others may speak with you, look inside of you, spend time with you, observe you, and empathize with you. They may infer, speculate, assume, and do whatever else is cognitively feasible to know you and how you feel. They may even get close to obtaining an accurate perception of your inner life. But there is a line between you and them that is impossible to cross, a boundary, outside of which stands all but you and God, a necessary separation between yourself and their selves, without which there would be no such thing as a glorious self. The same is true of the bond between you and God, a divine thought of you and only you that cannot be penetrated by any other person.

Understand that this bond between you and God did not passively arise from the mind of an indifferent God, but from the mind of a compassionate God, not a divine compassion that suffers with you or for you but a divine compassion that draws you into a place where suffering does not exist, from a God who in one single, infinite breath of thought exhales you out of nothing but his goodness, a big intellectual bang of an endless expanding universe of divine and human adventure, harmony, and pleasure, hand in hand, heart in heart, and life in life. God is waiting for you to live from that bond, to understand it, to exploit it, to enjoy it, and to do something with it. This bond is not a matter of position or pronouncement. It is a living, dynamic relationship that should be forever growing inward, upward, and outward, always full of change, not in God but in you, a being who should always be becoming more and more like him by consuming more and more of his limitless life.

Within this bond is where the place of faith resides and nowhere else—no Palestinian mountain top, no sanctuary filled with holy relics from the past, no nave surrounded by iconography, no ancient paved pathway to Calvary, and no empty tomb adorned with sacred symbols. None of this is to say that no powerful or valuable experience may take place within a believer at any of those venues. Rather, it is to say that the faith, hope, and love of the believer, their identity and worth, the idea of them within the mind of God, emerge from the bond between them and God, an intimate empiricism of human being and divine being where every moment and place of their life is sacred. Although the divergent experiences of transcending the worst conditions with quiet courage and vast perspective, or succumbing to unfavorable circumstances with a tireless timidity and incapacious vision are transitory but inevitable realities of our human freedom as they randomly materialize within our lives as they did within the life of Jesus, our bond with the creator is the mustard seed of a superlative reality that overshadows our deciduous experiences of victory or defeat, absolves us of any duty to adhere to the impotency of the explicative song and dance of theologians, and summons us to engage the triune God with all of our being. This engagement is not just within the institutionalized sacred time and place of the worship service, but when and where our lives are actually lived. Our life in God is much more than having convictions about interpretations of specific historical events or living within the confinements of what Jesus said or did. It is to see, seize, and live by the ultimate truth of our being that came from a gracious thought of the holy Trinity with the same intensity, significance, and meaning of love as Jesus the man embodied.

The fruits of the bond must be relinquished and bequeathed to others. If the harvest of God's life within us is not shared, it rots. He did not intend for us to accumulate the yield of his bond with us, but for us to give it away as he does. This is how our unique bond with God transforms our lives. The divine idea of change itself is a giving away—a gift that transfigures the giver into the holiness of God.

If some reject the bond between you and God because

they think it is unscriptural or fails to satisfy any canonical criterion, then you should "let the dead bury their dead"[6] and move on. They will have an eternity to catch up. On the other hand, as you become aware of this everlasting bond, there likely will be mistakes along the way in your understanding of the bond or in the direction you need to go. But no need to be afraid. God will redeem you from those mistakes and missteps. Otherwise, he would be neither good nor God.

Lord, this is my testimony. I suppose that if I had been a village priest in the north of France during the early eighteenth century, I may have been known as Father Meslier,[7] a remarkable but despondent atheist who had abandoned Christianity before he had become a priest and endeavored to demolish it with his last testament. I have no desire to renounce Christianity, but my frustration with its doctrines of unbelief in the truth and goodness of your character creates within me a soft heart for the unbelievers. I have a sense that atheistic or agnostic convictions are less counterfeit and contain more malleable material for you to engage than much of Christian conviction. The

---

6 Luke 9:60.

7 Jean Meslier was an eighteenth-century French priest who renounced Christianity.

personal declaration that no God exists, or that there is no way to definitively know one way or the other, in each case putting aside any philosophical incoherency, is inceptive, simplistic, and undarkened by overcast skies of nauseating, elitist theological explanation.

Christian conviction and its content subsume an irrationally complex and unbelievable narrative: Rivalries between divine love and wrath and between divine justice and mercy lie dormant, hibernating deep within the heart of God during a *perichoretic* winter until the springtime of creation when supposedly man makes one wrong choice of prideful independence and sin enters the void. This action causes God to recede, and a new species of humanity is born of the father of lies. The entire universe falls and groans; violence begets violence; destruction, disease, and death become the tragic epic of the new creatures until the divine dormancy ends. Then, God's love and wrath and justice and mercy prepare for battle; a lake bursts into flames; hell is born. The Trinitarian council of infinite goodness and wisdom convenes. The only begotten Son of God steps into the breach to absorb the full wrath and justice of God while nailed to a cross; love and mercy smile; Christianity and theology come forth. It is in this moment that an eternal choice must be made, either by God or by man, while heaven and hell await their new companions. Man sighs.

I believe there are many Christians who feel no sedative quality from this tale, who see this not as an "opiate of the people"[8] but as laughable and infuriating at once, who think this biography of God and man is engorged with the debris of a fatigued and diminutive imagination whose ideas of the love, goodness, and beauty of God cannot flourish beyond anything not carved from inspired texts. Dear God, if the Christian story is true and the eternal choice is for me to make or my lot has already been cast with the unchosen, then permit me to be the first hurled into the cauldron of incendiary judgment, an ironic reversal of what it means for the last to be first. If, on the other hand, the Christian story is true but I have already been chosen by you, then I hope to be the largest antagonist of this disgusting narrative and doctrine forever.

---

8   Karl Marx.

CHAPTER 7

The Finish

Ironically, today is Good Friday. Though I feel there's more to say, my prayer must come to an end. I have just returned from a church service where the crucifixion was glorified in a traditional solemn setting. Black cloths subdued the resplendence of the liturgical utensils, signifying the three hours of darkness surrounding your son's death. Musical instruments remained silent, only congregational voices of prayer and song graced the nave and sanctuary. Pensive reflections and emotional austerity enveloped the hearts and faces of the assembly. The sermon ensued.

The historically settled and safeguarded interpretation of the cross was poignantly conveyed with the unfathomable heaviness of that moment when the severity of divine and human distress finally surrendered to your decree of bloodshed. At that instant, the minister declared that the sin of all humanity, from the most innocuous to the most iniquitous, had been taken away by the Lamb of God, forever removed from your mind. Justice and mercy engaged the other but both were victorious. Wrath and love came face-to-face but both rejoiced.

The message would have been incomplete if the messenger had not labored to induce within the assembly a sense of culpability, a feeling that each of us had played our part in sending Christ to the cross, that the road to Calvary had been partially paved by our own wrongs, and that the two-thousand-year interval between my existence and his body nailed to blood-soaked wood above the blood-soaked ground had been bridged by my sin. Deep sadness and remorse were the intended effect.

But it was of no use. I had abandoned that spent vision of God, not because it had been exhausted, which anything true of you must be inexhaustible by definition, but because it is false. Christianity wants us to believe that nothing but the cross can occupy the uttermost place of divine and human centrality. The climactic event of all human history and futurity, the decisive moment between you and man, and yet further still, beyond the accessible region of human intellect where divine judgments and decrees originate, that is, the very heart of the triune God, the crucified Christ was the solution to the problem of sin and death, justice and mercy, love and wrath. The occasion of suffering and death of the perfectly innocent on intersecting planks of wood effects the divine adjustment required for reconciliation of a broken world with a holy God. It's as though Christianity were saying that we have a transactional God, a God bound by the logic of a financial exchange, a God who must negotiate, manage, and settle the terms of a purchase and sale. But ultimately, in order to transact and balance the eternal accounts, God must hurt and kill one of his own substance, the human form of the second person of the Trinity.

I wish we would see that to believe that you, the God above and beyond every other god, could have excluded us from your perennial presence, from your love, from your aesthetic purposes of creation, from your peace, from your beauty, and from your unqualified delight of having brought us forth from the womb of your heart, but instead look upon our hopeless condition of sin with a triumphant mercy summoned by the wounds of Christ, bearing your full outrage and justice in a spectacular display of glory, is to believe a lie. I wish we would see that to derive any sense of internal peace from such an irrational theology is an agitation of weightless froth, a massless superficiality that sustains nothing. It would take only an infant step of faith to grasp the gift of yourself, an imperishable outpouring of love, fellowship, and delight, and move closer to our perfectly devoted and unimaginably intimate father. We must return to our natural home, shed the human concoctions of atonement through suffering and other moronic blueprints of salvation, and escape the self-induced mirage that to reject such atonement teachings is to damn one's soul to an irreversible destiny of eternal agony and loneliness. I wish we would accept the truth that to repudiate the church's largest lie ever conceived draws us nearer to you, not away from you.

I do not deny that there's not a single page of this prayer without some form of verbal abuse. Although I seek no justification for the berating of the believer, your son's explosive and piercing vituperation during his earthly life is not without apostolic predicate. But, in my case, I strongly suspect that the origin of my invective against Christianity is more of a personality trait than spiritual clairvoyance.

Nevertheless, to the extent any of us can understand a trace of your truth—and I believe we can, otherwise creation would have been desperately directionless—we can understand that you create, love, forgive, and save unconditionally, without any prerequisite of violent maneuvers to resolve and overcome the problem of sin. Indeed sin doesn't present a divine dilemma. This is far closer to the truth of your character than any ecclesiastical explanation for the necessity of the cross. Moreover, to foreclose any subtle attempt at smuggling in some meaning of the cross through other historical Christ events, I believe that your nature to bestow uncovenanted mercy upon humanity required no particular divine action of any kind, whether the incarnation, life, or resurrection of Christ. It is your nature to forgive. The inquiry begins and ends there. The subject is closed. Any person who finds the matter too simplistic does not believe and know the God you are.

To say it another way, it is irresponsible, reckless, and immoral to hold the belief by virtue of any authority, whether revelatory or otherwise, that you are murderous by nature, or that pain, suffering, or any other ferocity is a feature of your being. As a further boundary of religious ingenuity, to characterize anything unconscionable as a paradox of truth castigates simple and authentic faith. There is no paradox between you and us.

The Gospels record a number of instances of your incarnate son indicating his foreknowledge of the crucifixion, his thought that some sort of ransom was required, his feeling that the brokenness of his body and the shedding of his blood were not only inevitable but also necessary. The Gospels report that Jesus viewed the gruesomeness of his end as establishing a new arrangement between you and us and that the difficult and desolate walk to the cross on the hill was an intentional relinquishment, on his part, of an imperforated blanket of surrender, without any political or religious "taking" by Roman authority or Jewish priesthood. It is of no consequence whether Christ actually said these things or whether the words or the ideas they represent were only later apostolic reflections. Here, however, I say my prayer under the assumption that the Gospels record the words of your son with absolute accuracy.

I believe that, to the extent our Lord spoke of a Trinitarian requirement for his own bloodshed and death as a condition of your mercy, as an appeasement of your wrath, as a satisfaction of your justice, as a payment of ransom, as a discharge of divine retribution, as obedience to your will or as an initiation of anything new in heaven or on earth, your son spoke in error. His feelings and convictions would have been misguided, though his heart remained pure and his obedience unyielding. This should not sound as blasphemous or dangerous to Christians as it may appear.

God, is it sin to be mistaken? Is it evil to misunderstand or be confused? Is imperfect knowledge or vision a breach of your law? I believe your answer is no. For the incarnation to have any meaning, Christ must have learned in the same manner as we do, with an abundance of mistakes and changes along the way.

Those questions were really designed to temporarily pacify the yearning of the believer who thinks that Christ, to be truly and fully human, must have possessed no sin as the Scriptures testify. The significance of that doctrine has vanished from my theological repertoire. It appears to me, Father, that there is no veridical reason why your son must have entered our predicament with no contamination, whether through the virgin birth or some other miraculous manner, and then lived a life without a single transgression.

The customary explanation offered by the church is that you needed to put to death a perfect man who knew no sin so that forgiveness could be called up from Trinitarian profundities and released upon us. My whole prayer rejects this degeneracy of your character. The church's explanation is morally bankrupt, and any Christian who does not see this sees very little of your ways, thoughts, and nature. They see a God who has become disabled by our sin, a God who became indebted to our transgressions, a God who must summon from his infinite expanse ways of dealing with human iniquity that are unthinkable to one with only an elementary understanding of your love and goodness. Who is sovereign—you or our sin?

This is high-stakes theology, but the doctrine of sin seems, for the most part, ill-conceived as a normative description, excessively dramatic as a narrative of rebellion, blame, and guilt, and overly consequential as a venue of eternal punishment, all converging to produce a depraved anthropology. I don't intend to diminish evil's brutal reality, especially the magnitude of evil witnessed in the twentieth century and in the beginning of this century.

The manifestations of evil can be strange, mysterious, and difficult to comprehend. At times, evil may appear to be a deprivation of goodness, a perversion of being, rational, irrational, motivated, unmotivated, civilized, uncivilized, isolated, communal, and even pedagogic. But I see sin more as a reflection of a broken ontology than as a deviation from a holy standard of external practice. I do not mean "broken" in the sense of a violent destruction of being where not even a shadow of goodness survives. I mean "broken" in the sense of a listless separation from you, a turning away more so than a turning against. Sin is not so much missing the mark as it is missing you, a disengagement of our unique being from your own, a refusal or reluctance to embrace, to explore, to feel, and to live from your heart-thought of each of us. Sin fundamentally disrupts our intrinsic belonging where every parochial moment of experience is christened with a harmonic relevancy.

Christianity's traditional understanding of sin's nature stresses a willful rebellion of humanity against you followed by a voluminous accumulation of blame and guilt. It's a volitional assertion of pride, a malicious declaration of independence from you, nothing short of obtaining full possession of unobstructed autonomy to do as we please without the slightest deference to you. Presumably this seminal disposition of rivalry infected all of humanity. It categorically changed the human species into guilty anarchists who are devoid of your life-giving spirit and who now must be arraigned, judged, and sentenced to eternal punishment.

I believe that this dramatic vision of sin, with all of its theatrical hyperbole, provides a constant source of funding for the otherwise indigent doctrine of substitutionary atonement. More fully, the doctrines of sin and substitutionary atonement endow each other with their respective figments and fallacies about your nature and our own. The more corrupt our nature, the more profound your intolerable holiness. The greater your wrath, the greater our guilt. This sort of vicious reciprocity culminates in the ultimate justification of both doctrines—our categorical decadence requires the cross and the cross establishes our categorical decadence.

In recent decades, much of Christian concern about sin is really not about sin at all but its consequences, particularly those of an eternal nature. With so much needless anxiety over the two possible destinations, one of happiness and the other of horror, the gospel message has been designed to induce an impetuous rebirth (or increase head count) with no regard for how the converted should fight and resist evil. So long as the spontaneous decision is made to accept the vicarious death of Christ on the cross, the heavenly ticket is punched and the believer may recline in peace, free of all distress and despair over the consequences of sin.

In the end, though, however one may understand the nature of sin—nihilistic, banal, demonic, separation, or insurrectionary—the death of your son, itself an inevitable consequence of sin, does nothing against it. The cross has no power over evil. It does not subvert the potency of wickedness or rehabilitate the human condition. The force of this truth is most compelling when one considers a person who is as close to absolute corruption as divinely possible, someone who appears to have no conscience whatsoever, no regard for human life, their own or another's, and who is virtually indistinguishable from pure evil. This is a person who seems beyond recovery. This is a person who we believe deserves a lifetime of punishment when we view them from a frenzied state, but when we are in a more pastoral state, we think they deserve complete annihilation. In your eyes, oh God, this destitute person does not need the divine death of Christ. They need the divine life of Christ. The forfeiture of your son's earthly life on the cross does nothing for this man's condition. It does not change him. It does not make him better. It makes nothing right. Infinitely more important, it changes neither you nor how you see him. Your boundless life is his only hope.

To hold with a death grip the belief that every drop of blood that rolled down the body of Christ, down the cross, and dried up in the ground pleased you, authorized the divine forgiveness of our sinful deeds, or allowed you to see our broken condition in a new godly reality lays waste to your character. These Christians, who perhaps are just trying to fit in, would do almost anything to protect this belief, ingrained as it is in their hearts and inextricably preserved in their minds. Their authentic faith has all but been relinquished to the supremacy of Scripture and two thousand years of consensus among theologians, teachers, and holy men and women of your church. I know. I was one of those Christians.

Even Christ himself questioned whether he would

find true faith on the earth when he returns.[1] No account in the Synoptics illustrates this quality of faith more strikingly than the encounter between Christ and the Canaanite woman. When she had been not only ignored by the disciples and personally dismissed by Christ but also characterized by him as a dog in contrast to the Israelites as the chosen and privileged people of God and to whom Christ's mission was exclusively dedicated, the woman, whose deepest desire was her daughter's health, disregarded our Lord's commission and its theological implications as irrelevant to her, an ineligible human mutt, and insisted that Christ toss her a handful of the crumbs of life. He recognized immediately that, although her faith was as far away as it could be from theological truth as he understood it, the faith of the Canaanite woman was remarkable. It was one of only two times in all four Gospels when Christ distinguished a person's faith as great.

What made her faith great? Because a thousand years of an abundant religious tradition about a new divine kingdom, free of oppression but full of triumph, one of the fundamental themes of the entire Old Testament, championed by numerous kings and prophets, and

---

1 Luke 18:8.

believed by your son, was of no consequence to her simple need and faith. This unelected woman, having no choice in her birth, upbringing, culture, or religion and standing outside of the messianic blessing, says to Christ: "Fix it." That was the depth of her theology.

There are many Christians who silently accommodate doubts about biblical authority, who are unmoved by centuries of ecclesiastical consensus, and have not allowed cognitive biases to impede their rationality. They do not endorse substitutionary atonement. Yet there are other Christians who are not sure what to make of the doctrine of the cross because they feel the dissension between the goodness of your character and the divine exchange of the innocent for the guilty, between a justice of divine fairness and a justice of divine judgment that the cross implies.

Now, at last, I come to my deepest prayer. My heart kneels before you with the most adored doctrine of Christianity in my hands—the atoning work of Christ on the cross.

I pray that you would repudiate it, utterly.

I pray that you would give us the fearlessness to remove from our minds all theories of atonement and to dispose of them to where they belong—the refuse pile of human theological contrivance.

I pray that you would liberate our hearts from the

encumbrances of perverted truth, debilitating falsehoods, and defrauding fear that emerge from forced and factitious meanings of the cross.

I pray that you would extinguish all of those meretricious exhilarations that have attached themselves to the lies of the cross within the emotional life of Christianity and that you would fill the sentimental void with the honest and sound feelings that come from trusting in and feasting upon the truth of your character.

I pray that you would open the eyes of our souls to see your goodness with clarity. You are a God who looks upon and loves his creatures with the infinite fullness of God the Father, God the Son, and God the Holy Spirit, with no subterfuge or pretension. No image of the crucified and risen Christ suspended between a holy God and sinful man belongs to a God who always does the uttermost for every person, not vicariously or by intersession, but directly, heart to heart, being to being, a God who never abrogates or abandons any person, even the true man Christ as he hung nailed to the cross. You are a God whose love requires no catalyst of punishment or pain to mobilize its actuality, a God whose mercy does not demand the redness of blood, even of the Lamb of God, as a divine stimulation, but is always already on the move, and a God whose impeccable righteousness and relentless justice demand every person be righteous and just as you are; in other words, to be good, loving, and merciful as you are.

I pray that you would break into our souls and dispel our staid belief that we are healed by the wounds of Christ. Expose it for what it truly is—a curse, a disgrace, an arraignment of your character, an impeachment of your love, justice, and mercy. You, oh God the Father, did not bleed your son dry to pay our debts. Wake us up from this crisis of unbelief. As this twenty-first century advances, does not every Christian who witnesses the immense scale of global violence stand utterly horrified? But when it comes to you, the source of all goodness, peace, and beauty, our horror of the violent cross becomes our joy, gratitude, and blessing. Violence among humanity evokes our disgust, but violence among the Godhead evokes our admiration.

Oh, my God, what multigenerational and complex network of irrational and delirious thinking is needed to justify the necessity for your son's crucifixion—expositions that from beginning to end are false, thoroughly deprived of the reality of who you are. For centuries we have, with little hesitation or misgiving, inhaled institutional authority for how you move within the depths of humanity to redeem and reconcile, and placidly approved institutional doctrine with its customary dogmatic exclusivity, and believed that only the church may open the gates to the kingdom of your presence with her keys as though you would abandon a creature of your own heart as irrevocably dead to you. And now, having been full for so long with theological debris, I feel that we have lost our divine gift of spiritual curiosity, that intense inquisitiveness about you, that simple disposition of mind that says: "I want to understand you for myself."[2] When questions and doubts arise during our Christian experience, we are admonished not to inquire of you, but to search the Scriptures and traditions, to become reacquainted with that timeworn path lined with colorless tombs of deceased doctrine that leads us to the top of the hill where, we are told, you made peace with us by the cross of suffering and death. Our theology becomes domesticated as we dwell in our theistic encasements of familiarity and safety, swaddled with our holy texts and traditions. But this domesticated theology censors our spirit of inquiry and imagination of you and

---

[2] The spirit of wonder that I wish to capture is wonderfully portrayed in Chapter 3 of Exodus where Moses personally encounters God for the first time in the burning bush on the top of Mount Horeb. Before the official place and practice of worship had been institutionalized and the voluminous laws were laid down, Moses, understandably amazed and bewildered by the burning but unconsumed bush, says: "I will now turn aside and see this great sight . . . " Exodus 3:3 (NKJV).

habituates our God-thoughts. Rather than venture anything or anywhere with you, we prefer to stay in our cribs staring up at our tired religious mobiles and teething on our poisonous pacifiers. Give us the courage, dear God, to grow up and out from our spiritual infancy.

I pray that you would heal us from our unbelief. That you would help us see the God you truly are, that you would reanimate us with your abundant life, and that you would restore our thirst for others or anything other than ourselves, and revive our spirited passion to be true, more so than to know what truth is—Pilate's injudicious question to Jesus.[3]

Finally, while we are in those moments when we seem indistinguishable from the mass of humanity, oscillating between extinguishment and endless obscurity, when we are invisible to the world, when freedom seems empty and we have a dreadful sense of the inescapable necessity to fulfill the ceaseless demands of family and vocation, when we wish we had a feeling of despair or loneliness because it's better than a feeling of nothingness, or when we are overcome by the memory that what has already unfolded in our lives seems valueless and are overwhelmed by the feeling that we will not be able to do anything meaningful

---

3   John 18:38.

in the future, I pray that you would strengthen our labors to explore, see, and believe that the truth of each of us, without exception, has its origin within a unique chamber of your heart.

It has been said, "He of whom God thinks, lives."[4] It should also be said, "He of whom God loves, lives," for God's thought and love are one and the same. Your thought is eternally invariable. It does not recede because of sin. No belief or unbelief, no perspective or system of thought adopted by us can affect your thought of us. It cannot evaporate because of our unresponsiveness. It is forever fixed. If such were not the case, if our Christianity, heresy, or atheism in any way changed how you think of us, then you would not be God. If the strength of our rebellion or the coldness of our indifference could transform your invariable thought into variable thought, then you would not be God.

The significance of this truth is complemented by another truth: The diversity of your thought expressed in the creation of humanity is a shadow of the diversity within the Trinity itself. Each person is born of a unique thought of yours, different from your thought of any other person. Such person's nature, life, purpose,

---

4 MacDonald, *Unspoken Sermons: Series I*, 159.

meaning, worth, freedom, divinization, and glory—in a word, beauty—are to be found in that thought and only there. Because your thought is different for each person, a person's beauty is different from every other person's. Only that person, and no other, can express that unique beauty, can fill in the distinctive heavenly pattern with their own changes in pitch, tone, and cadence, and can sing the eternal verse written just for them by your mind. Only each person can articulate your eternal message conceived just for them, and clothe that divine thought with human utterances. Each person is a unique voice and word of God.

But this beatific vision of each person's life does not culminate there. In fact, there's no culmination for any person who participates in your life—no summit of personal development or zenithal state of humanity. The participation expands perpetually through unceasing advances of enrichment to more and more of you. But those everlasting accumulations of rapturous experience with you will by no means be for the exclusive enjoyment of the individual. In heaven they will be shared with the rest of humanity; they must be shared, for no person can live without them, not out of necessity but for pure delight. To me, God, this is the true body of Christ—the endless exchange of narrative and song in the ecstasy and enchantment of fellowship, harmony, and laughter with you and creation, without any interruption of a whisper of selfishness or ambition.

This is paradise. All purpose, meaning, and substance are on the surface. Depthlessness, openness, exteriority, and aesthetics will reign. Everywhere we look, everything we think or do, and every feeling we have will be beautiful, all to the delight and pleasure of you. All desire or need for theological explanation will cease, including my own. It's no wonder why my favorite Old Testament promise is when Jeremiah said, "No longer will a man teach his neighbor, or a man his brother, saying 'Know the Lord,' because they will all know me, from the least of them to the greatest, declares the Lord."[5]

To complete my paradisal speculations, the Gospel of John says, "Jesus wept."[6] I believe it. Who can be genuinely human but not weep? My vision of you and my hope in you, however, do not reside there. Instead, the thing that keeps me grounded, as they say, the truth that satisfies my soul that all is well and will continue to be well with the Father, the Son, and the Holy Spirit is what the Gospels fail to say: "Jesus laughed," a genuine expression

---

5 Jeremiah 31:34.
6 John 11:35.

of merriment or a display of cheerfulness, not the chuckle of a docetic Jesus who had duped some to believe in his physicality as is portrayed in certain gnostic gospels. Who can be genuinely human but not laugh? You created this explosive and spontaneous emotion. It's a revelation of what you're like. It's a lubricant for life's toils and travails. Does there exist a more precious sight than to see an infant overcome with laughter? What better remedy for the ills of Christian theology than for the church to set aside the deadly seriousness of its disposition, the urgency with which it sees its own significance, and its venomous message about you to the world, and to allow itself to be conquered and speechless for a time by laughter? Christianity should get used to the idea that heaven will be filled with laughter.

One last thought before I go that may be more fundamental than laughter. I know this question is a flawless example of nonsense, but if you were to ask me what is the deepest part of you, I would say "reason," because that's all I need to know for now. I could figure out the rest some time during eternity. To me, this is what it comes down to: Are you a rational or an irrational God? Christianity has shown the world the depth of feculent belief that can be carpentered in the name of a loving God—after all,

"For God so loved the world . . . "[7] I don't think that would have been the case if Christianity had believed that you were a reasonable God, for reason would not send an innocent man to a cross of suffering and death. This is not to say that there's no mystery with you or nothing about you that we cannot comprehend. Personally, when it comes to the idea of divine mystery, I can take it or leave it. But if Christianity insists on having an element of mystery within the Godhead, then it should shove the mystery outside of the relationship between the maker and the made. There, it does not belong.

My God, my God, as I sit unclothed in my boat in a slough that I have come to call "monk slough," I feel I have said to you all I can about the suffering and death of your son. Unquestionably, this prayer of a Homeric "noble fury"[8] contains many inconsistencies, flaws, and reckless assertions. Nevertheless, I see no return to the traditional understanding of the cross. When I began to question the veracity of those atonement explanations and what they say about your character, the theological litter began to clear. There was no going back. The ship

---

7 John 3:16.
8 Homer, the ancient Greek poet, began *The Iliad* with the fury of Achilles.

had become unmoored and began to sail against a strong wind. It wasn't long before the old land off the stern had melted away and new land appeared off the bow. The land was alive and lush, not with the spectrum of trees and flowers, but with the immaculacy and simplicity of reasonableness and sensibility, a quality of childlikeness that we all know, tender and tenacious. I feel closer to the spirit of Christ in the new homeland. I do hope that Christians will in due time cross the rough waters of their own making and come ashore. They would love it.

I also hope that Christians would put themselves in the imaginary encounter with you that I mentioned in the preface to this prayer. As they look into the eyes of your being, I pray that they would see you as you truly are, an endless excellency beyond any of our theological investigations or constructs. These obsolete ideas are only visions encrusted with mesozoic scales of extinct belief that synthesize your holiness as wrath, justice as judgment, majesty as retribution, and your glory as suffering into a terrifying divine autobiography of violence. This foolish theology seeks to display the dreadfulness of your sovereignty and the unintelligibility of your pleasure. I pray that they would see all of your attributes as manifestations of your love and reasonableness in the creation, forgiveness, and restoration of all humanity, a peaceful divine autobiography of pure delight, harmony, and beauty.

What would we say when that ultimate encounter with you occurs? Probably not much at first. But after we regain our breath, after each of us receives the completely unexpected but then realizes that it was what we really always desired—a unique identity, aspiration, and meaning ready to unfold for the entire universe to see, a living revelation of you that only we can live and reveal—we'll have much to say because our faith will be like the faith of the Canaanite woman. It will be simple joy.

What will you say to us? If my perception of you in this prayer approaches the truth of your character, if these thoughts contain only a seed of divine actuality, then you would not and could not say to any human being: "I never knew you. Away from me, you evildoers."[9] Or the more ruthless adjudication: "Depart from me, you who are cursed, into the eternal fire prepared for the devil and his angels."[10]

It is a divine impossibility for creatures to end in a harsh and hopeless state at the hand of their creator, no matter how much we desire to see the worst of humanity

---

9 Matthew 7:23.
10 Matthew 25:41.

endure an unmerciful fate and no matter that those sayings came directly from Christ himself according to the Gospel of Matthew. The glory of our creation, in your mind, is that it's all or nothing. There is no compromise or concession within the Godhead. Your idea of each of us will be fully realized in spite of whatever else you permit to happen.

There may be nothing for you to say to us. No explanation by you will be necessary. No justification of any historical event will be required of you. Once we see you, we will understand what must be understood and everything else will be forgotten. Then, we will begin our eternal journey with you and each other.

For now, all of us must realize that our distance from the truth is measured more by what we do than by what we know. It is finished. Amen.

Glossary

For convenience, I have provided this glossary for less commonly used words that I chose to use in this prayer. Most of the definitions in this glossary were derived from Dictionary.com.

acclimatization: to become accustomed to a new environment.

achromatic: free from color.

anthropomorphic: ascribing human attributes to a deity.

antinomic: a contradiction between two laws.

aphotic: lightless.

apocryphal: questionable or fake.

apostate: heretical or nonconformist.

axiomatic: self-evident.

banality: devoid of freshness or originality.

cacophonous: having a harsh sound.

cadaverous: corpse-like.

caliginous: dim or dark.

castigate: to criticize severely.

cataractal: impenetrable to light.

chromatically: pertaining to colors.

clairvoyance: intuitive knowledge.

deciduous: annual shedding of leaves; transitory.

decrepitude: a feeble state.

deleterious: harmful or damaging.

denude: to make bare.

depredatory: ravage.

desultory: lacking in consistency.

diacritic: unique.

dimorphism: the occurrence of two forms distinct in coloration or other features among animals or plants of the same species.

dissonance: discord.

docetic: relating to an early Christian teaching that the suffering and death of Christ only appeared to be, but in fact were not, real.

efficacious: capable of having the desired effect.

effluence: outward flows.

emblematize: to serve as a symbol.

enigmatic: a puzzling situation.

enmity: a hostile feeling.

entropy: inevitable degeneration.

equanimity: emotional stability.

exegetical: explanatory.

exiguous: meager or small.

expletory: a profane expression.

feculent: fecal matter.

flaccid: soft and limp.

geodesic: the geometry of curved surfaces.

gossamer: a fine cobweb seen on grass or bushes.

immanence: indwelling.

immolation: a sacrifice.

incantation: the chanting of words.

incendiary: inflammatory.

inceptive: beginning.

inchoate: incomplete.

incipiency: in an initial stage.

indurate: having been made hard or enduring.

ineffability: incapable of being described in words.

inerrantist: a person who believes that the Bible is free from error.

inextirpable: inerasable.

inextricably: incapable of being disentangled.

intorsion: inward rotation around an axis.

intransigency: inflexibility.

invective: an insulting expression.

irremissible: unpardonable.

juridical: legal.

malignancy: tending to produce suffering or death.

mellifluous: smoothly flowing.

mendicancy: a person who lives by begging.

mendicity: beggarly.

meretricious: alluring by flashy attraction.

mesozoic: the era of the dinosaurs.

metastasize: to spread.

myopic: shortsighted.

neoteric: modern or new.

nimiety: overabundance.

novitiate: a beginner in a religious order.

oblation: offering.

ontological: based upon or relating to the nature of existence.

opulent: wealthy or affluent.

ossuary: a receptacle for the bones of the dead.

paradigmatic: an ideal model.

parochial: narrow in scope.

pendulous: hanging down loosely.

perennial: an indefinitely long time.

perichoresis: a Greek term that describes the mutual relationship of love among the persons of the Trinity.

perspicacity: a keen understanding.

placentary: fetal nourishment.

poignancy: emotionally intense or moving.

prattle: foolish talk.

precipitous: extremely steep.

predilection: a tendency to think favorably of something.

prismatic: bright.

prodigious: extraordinary in size or extent.

progenitor: ancestor.

propitiatory: satisfaction or conciliatory.

proselytistic: relating to recruiting in the religious area.

prostration: submission or extreme mental exhaustion.

pubescence: pre-adult or immature.

recalcitrance: rebellious or stubborn.

recapitulate: to repeat.

ruminant: contemplative.

saliency: prominence.

salvific: redemptive power.

sedimentary: the least valuable part of anything.

sedulous: diligent application or attention.

seminal: highly original.

sidereal: belonging to the stars.

sinusoidal: a wavelike curve.

soteriology: the doctrine of salvation.

subjugation: bringing under control.

suffuse: spread out.

Synoptics: the Gospels of Matthew, Mark, and Luke.

systematician: using a system.

tautology: needless repetition.

tenacious: holding fast.

tonic immobility: a natural state of paralysis of certain animals.

traverse: to pass over.

trepidation: fear or alarm.

vacuous: empty.

valence: the capacity of a person to react with or affect another in some special way.

vapid: dull or lacking life.

vassalized: made into a servant or slave.

venial: an excusable offense.

veridical: truthful.

vermicular: the movements of worms or maggots in rotting flesh.

vicissitude: changing phases or conditions.

vituperation: verbal abuse.

winnow: to blow upon.

Acknowledgments

I owe several lifetimes of pure gratitude to my wife, Blair, and my four children—Mallie, Taylor, Holly, and Miller—but not solely because of this prayer. The reflection and writing required for this prayer consumed massive amounts of solitary time. They sacrificed a great deal without a single grievance. I know there's more than one way to interpret that. I love them all, deeply.

Many, many thanks to Nancy, my secretary of more than thirty years. For the record, she fought me over every paragraph of the first draft and had to do most of the typing with her eyes closed.

My thoughts about the aesthetics of God's life in all of his Trinitarian splendor that appear throughout this prayer were shaped by the work of David Bentley Hart, especially his books *The Beauty of the Infinite—The Aesthetics of Christian Truth* and *The Doors of the Sea: Where Was God in the Tsunami?*

There were many places in this prayer where I had no idea of what to say or how to say it. The interior quietude

I needed to work through these obstacles came from the instrumental guitar music of John Danley.

For more than a decade I have been a member of the Wingfold email community, which is devoted to the life and work of George MacDonald. A special thanks to all the Wingfolders for their stimulating insights and discussions.

I am deeply indebted to Chris Lundberg who helped me to shape, redirect, rethink, develop, and connect many of the arguments in this book. He has great insight and a very deep understanding of theological issues.

Without Kelly Gwathney and Sarah Zink, there would have been no Chris. Thank you.

I owe much to Melissa Anne Wuske who clarified my thinking.

Additionally, thanks to Sheila Parr whose creativity radiates from the cover of this book.

Finally, I am incredibly grateful to all of the folks at Greenleaf who took a giant leap of faith to publish this book and whose professionalism is unparalleled. And, many special thanks to AprilJo Murphy, my chief editor at Greenleaf, who's an artisan at bringing simplicity out of obscurity while preserving the author's voice, and to Elizabeth Brown, my copy editor at Greenleaf, who has absolutely razor-sharp skills.

ABOUT THE AUTHOR

Timothy John Tracy is a corporate transactional lawyer with a career of more than thirty years at the firm of Balch & Bingham LLP in Birmingham, Alabama. Although he has no formal theological education or training, his hidden passion, cultivated for decades, has been to explore, question, and understand the character of God in a different but sensible manner. That passion, now exposed, will be a revelation to most who know him. They will be astonished that the idea of God has actually entered his mind. But he will insist that, as the Scriptures affirm and history bears witness, truth is not the exclusive domain of those with pedigree, profile, or brand. Tim lives in the Birmingham community with his wife and daughters.

www.ingramcontent.com/pod-product-compliance
Lightning Source LLC
Chambersburg PA
CBHW030443090526
44586CB00044B/603